The Laws of Success

A Spiritual Guide to Turning Your Hopes Into Reality

RYUHO OKAWA

IRH PRESS

BOOKS
IRH PRESS
New York

Library of Congress Cataloging-in-Publication Data

ISBN 13: 978-1-942125-15-0
ISBN 10: 1-942125-15-1

Printed in China

First Edition

Book Design: Jess Morphew
Cover image © Shutterstock / DVARG

CONTENTS

THREE

· · · · · · · ·

The Secrets of Successful Living

FOUR

· · · · · ·

The Keys to Succeeding in Business

SEVEN

....

The Path to
Ultimate Self-Realization

EIGHT

....

Success Principles
for Today's Leaders

The Laws of Success

PREFACE

In 1988, at the age of thirty-two, I published the first Japanese edition of this book under the title *The Philosophy of Modern Success: The Bible for the Elite Businessperson* through a publisher called Tsuchiya Shoten. I had founded Happy Science two years previously, and my recognition in the public eye had risen into prominence over the course of those two years. I have never read any other book that has offered a philosophy of success as extensive as the one I offer in this volume. For that reason, and because the topics made this an appropriate next book in the Laws series that we publish every year in Japan, I added this book in 2004 as the new, ninth volume in this series.

The passage of time has anything but dated this book's relevance; in fact, the passing of time has allowed the words in these pages to grow more universal and illuminating. Since this book was first published, its ideas have taken flight and catapulted Happy Science onto the stage of world religions. The first release foreshadowed my achievements since then, and these accomplishments validate my philosophy, making it clear that it is not just an empty theory.

This book boldly presents principles for succeeding in both our personal lives and our business lives. If you read this book during your twenties and thirties, you will surely have remarkable success in your life, and I eagerly encourage you to study these pages deeply. Readers in their forties or fifties and older may at first feel a pang of regret and then a tinge of remorse. But do not be let down, because the remainder of your life still holds possibilities for growth. There is still sufficient time for you to succeed, especially if you hold a managerial position, work as a business executive, are the breadwinner for your family, or are a mother raising children.

You might sense the confidence of a young genius pervading the entire book. If I were to meet myself back then today, I have no doubt that I would be deeply moved and struck with a great sense of awe. I am proud to have written this would-be classic at the young age of thirty-two and to have grown myself with this book in hand. It is my sincere hope that my readers will want to come back to this book time after time throughout their lives.

Ryuho Okawa
Founder and CEO
Happy Science Group

ONE

What Is True Success?

An Attractive Life

If you decided to pick up this book on finding success, you have probably, at some point, wondered what kind of life you were born to live and given this question a lot of thought. You may have found that, no matter how much you pursued an answer, life is such that the answer only grew more elusive. And perhaps the more deeply you penetrated, the more you discovered how much remained to be fathomed.

In our quest to understand what it means to attain success in life, what we ought to be most concerned with is how we ultimately wish to describe the final outcome of our lives. The question we should be asking is: When we look back on our lives, which word do we want to come to mind the most?

For example, if you were to choose a word like *unhappy* to express how you wish your life to ultimately turn out, this adjective alone would do plenty to tinge your life with misfortune and gloom. On the other hand, an opposite word, like *happy*, evokes rosy images of a delightful journey through life.

In this search to understand the essence of a successful life, I would like to begin by crowning *life* with the adjective *attractive*. I believe that searching for the qualities of life that my heart is naturally drawn to will eventually lead me to the essence of success.

What makes life attractive? There are a myriad of books these days that talk about how to achieve success. Their notion of an attractive life seems to be based on drawing the envy of those around us. But after poring through all those pages, I was left unconvinced by this idea. I couldn't shake the feeling that the lives of those who deeply appeal to us affect us in more ways than simply whetting our desires or piquing our curiosities. This search led me to three essential pillars.

The first pillar is originality. To live an attractive life, it is important that we make use of our time on earth in a way that is unique and authentic so that we can confidently call our lives our very own.

The second pillar is sheer joy. Our life should impart us with a sense of true pride and sheer joy and be a journey of meaning and purpose that brings us a sense of true fulfillment. It ought to bring many moments in which we are overcome with delight and happiness, time and time again.

The third pillar is a sense of unique contribution. We should feel that our lives have added something new and different to the world, that in this life we were able to bring a unique gift to the world.

When I consider these three pillars and think of the elements that make life attractive, I arrive at an essential truth about the essence of life and who we really are. The widespread trend of this modern age is to believe in a limited notion of human life. A lot of people in the world today believe in the idea that you only live once and then that'll be the end of everything.

Perhaps you or some of the people you know have spent their lives following this view of life as though it's only natural and just a self-evident truth.

But I have been baffled by the wide acceptance of this belief. Where is the allure in believing that we will perish forever upon the end of our mortal lives? This notion has continued to elude me. It is not my style to pressure anyone to accept what I personally hold to be true. But, at the end of the day, even if we only weigh the benefits against the disadvantages, the benefits of believing that we humans have eternal life far outweigh the disadvantages. Believing in an eternal life absolutely helps us live fuller lives.

I follow the timeless teaching of the saints and sages of times past, who time and time again taught humanity the truth about the everlasting nature of the human soul. And I also believe that we are blessed, on many an occasion, with mortal garbs that allow us to take journeys to this world.

Because I believe these things and know that my essence will live on forever, I am able to find meaning and purpose in the time I spend in this world. Since I believe that my true essence will continue eternally, I don't feel a desire to live only for myself. Instead, I would rather follow my true passion, which calls me to live in service to others. This is how the belief that our lives will truly never come to an end inspires us to make our lives truly attractive and meaningful.

When we consider the three pillars of an attractive life from the perspective of our eternal life, it becomes clear that our most important task is to draw on our unique inner essence to discover, invent, and conceive things that will be of worth to the world. Our true purpose is to create something fresh and original to enrich the lives of those who live in this new age.

I hope that you will share in my desire to conceive and create new things of value for the world to come.

A Blithe and Breezy Attitude

We may not have to look hard to find many people who have succeeded in creating very attractive lives. But I have discovered that only a few of these people have inspired my genuine envy and admiration. These are the kind of people who not only lead an attractive life, but also manage to maintain a bright and easy attitude throughout life.

What do these people have that allows them to be at ease and to live with poise? What gives them their blithe and breezy air? What is their secret? And why is this considered such a wonderful, attractive quality?

People who maintain a blithe and breezy attitude have two admirable traits.

First, living with a blithe and breezy attitude allows us to live with inner calm and composure. The ability to preserve our calm and divine poise, no matter what comes our way, is truly worth its weight in gold. What really brings us misery are the extreme oscillations of the mind—the ups and downs of emotions that can make us soar to joy in one moment and then crash down into the blues in the next. When we are able to move past ruffled emotions and find stillness in our mind, we can fully enjoy the happiness of an inner peace that resembles the smooth and placid ripples of the vast seas.

The second admirable trait of people with a bright and breezy attitude is that they never inflict pain or hurt upon others. I don't think I have ever seen a blithesome person ever behave unkindly toward others. Every time I observe someone committing a hurtful action, it confirms in my mind that the secret to making our world a better place has got to be increasing the number of people who carry a blithesome heart.

Those who have such a heart have an important quality that hints at how they manage to never bring others injury: they are skilled at letting go. Not everyone we know is going to share the same likes and dislikes as us. It is the same with our personal views and ideas: occasionally, in the course of conversation, people may refuse to accept our thoughts and opinions. When these occasions arise, people who possess a blithesome attitude are able to handle the tension as if by letting it just slip away. They are mindful not to take unpleasantries to heart or too seriously. They do their best to remain unruffled and let these things go. In this way, a blithe attitude gives us the power to make everyone's lives feel much more pleasant.

If we want to cultivate a blithesome attitude, the key is to cherish each and every day with gratitude. Life may feel like a very long journey, but when we look closely, it is actually the accumulation of one day upon the next. Our lives, therefore, depend on living each and every day with a bright and breezy heart. This means that we must not hold on to the discontents and dissatisfactions that we felt one day, two days, three days, six months, or as far back as a year ago, for if we do, we will never give our mind the freedom to be positive and calm.

We should encourage ourselves to resolve our problems within the span of each day. Then, we have no reason to carry any of our discontents or dissatisfactions on to the next day. This is the secret to preserving our ease and divine poise from day to day and through our whole lives. Maintaining a blithesome and breezy mind in the face of life's troubles and discords is part of the challenge and purpose of human life.

A Heart of Love

If you are like me, you may have spent some time perusing books about how to achieve success. These books offer useful knowledge, including personal success stories, theories of success, and how-tos. But most of them don't talk about an essential element of true success that, without it, our achievements turn out to be shallow. This element is love.

Visible signs of progress such as wealth and profit, the growth and expansion of a business enterprise, or advancement up the corporate ladder are, indeed, essential components of success. But I believe that there is much more to true success than just these outward achievements. Another vital component is the element of love. Without love to guide us, we wouldn't know how to bring true happiness to humanity or what needs to be done to bring others joy.

Can you really feel proud of yourself if your achievements bring others disappointment and misery? Will you truly feel satisfied by simply reaping rewards for yourself? Are outward results all you need to feel truly successful?

I believe that success should be something that arises from a heart that burns with compassion and love. So-called success that is empty of love is also empty of true success.

What is vital is that you cultivate a constant, abiding heart of love. Over time, your heart of love will help you accomplish more and more good for the world as it touches, inspires, and uplifts more and more people.

What are the qualities of a heart of love? And what can we do to find our own inner source of love to make our success authentic and real?

One essential aspect of the heart of love is a constant and eager interest in the world and in people. This is a quality that all truly successful people have in common. To truly love humanity, we must have an inexhaustible desire to understand as much as possible about people and societies. To feel true love and compassion for the people around us, we must cultivate the ability to perceive them deeply.

The second important aspect of a heart of love is deep introspection and self-knowledge. Knowing who you really are and unearthing the remarkable aspects of yourself are indispensable to maintaining a heart of love. To truly love others, we need to have discovered our own remarkable qualities. We need to know how to recognize the outstanding aspects of our own souls to be able to find the outstanding aspects of the souls of others.

Each time we are able to look upon ourselves with warmth and tenderness, we learn to look upon others with the same heart of compassion and kindness. This is why knowing who you really are is so important to cultivating a heart of love.

The third aspect of a heart of love is the constant desire to give ever more love. In this sense, progress is intrinsic to love.

True love is never truly satisfied by small acts of goodwill or small achievements, because, by its nature, it never truly feels that it has accomplished enough for others. True love always holds a wish to advance and progress further in the work that it can do.

To sum up, to cultivate a heart of love is to keep discovering more and more remarkable aspects of yourself. It is to cultivate as many meaningful relationships as possible with those around you and to find and nurture the extraordinary qualities lying within them. And finally, it is to never allow these desires to come to an end.

A Sense of the Eternal

So far, I have talked about the qualities that characterize people who are within just a stone's throw of success: they are accomplished and have attractive lives, they have a blithe and breezy disposition, and they carry a constant heart of love.

But now, I would like to describe what we will find within success. When I think about success, I think of the one thing that success should always bring us: an abiding sense of the eternal.

No matter how much effort we devote to advancing our work and careers, cultivating personal growth, and nurturing our relationships, unless these endeavors bring us a sense of the eternal, they may turn out to be frail and shallow.

For example, we may pour our passion into our work or other endeavors every day, but I wonder how many of us have considered whether the purpose we derive from our activities give us hopes of something everlasting? Do you see or feel passing moments of the eternal during the time you devote to work? If you don't, then even if you do succeed, your own heart may regard your success as frail and insubstantial. That is why the word *eternal* is so vital to true success. Even if we consider the attainment of happiness to be the attainment of success, our happiness will feel shallow and fragile without a feeling of the eternal.

What do we do to feel an abiding sense of the eternal? Experiences of the eternal are not easy to come by, to say the least. They are but divine moments that sweep in upon us quite unawares. They are feelings that we cannot use our own volition to attain, as we would like. They are fleeting glimpses of the world of eternity that we catch in the midst of constant day-to-day endeavor.

Is there anything we can do to invite these moments of eternity? There is a basic condition that helps us maintain a sense of the eternal, and that is knowing what all our day-to-day effort is for.

The word *eternal*, I believe, is kindred to the word *God*. And by thinking about the eternal nature of God, we gain an understanding of the everlasting nature of human life and, therefore, our eternal purpose.

We human beings came forth into this world from eternity—from God—and it is our destiny to return into eternity in the course of time. That original universe of everlastingness is a world that our true essence has been a part of forever. So this physical, evanescent world can give us a sense of futility and forlornness.

When we feel this emptiness, what can we do to fill the hole? It is difficult to attain a sense of eternity and catch glimpses into eternal life when, in reality, we are confined within the physical life of the present. It is also a monumental undertaking to try to create a legacy, within these circumstances, that will truly last forever.

The answer that the ancients and all of humanity through

history have arrived at is *immortality*. No one has ever managed to find a way to live eternally in this world, but our predecessors found many ways to leave behind legacies that have stood the test of time long after they have left this world.

All through history, we humans have poured our life and passion into this longing to transcend death. This basic human desire was the driving force that inspired us to raise towering monuments that still stand to this day, to paint masterpieces that continue to adorn our halls, and to leave behind vast bodies of knowledge that nourish new minds every day. All remarkable feats of human endeavor came from this simple wish to transcend our mortal existence, to set ourselves free from the limits of time and corporeal existence, and to soar into the skies of the everlasting.

Today, the seat of this desire for immortality continues on within us, and we express it through new endeavors, for example, by creating corporate enterprises and working to make them grow and prosper. We don't expect corporations to last forever, but we strive to keep them alive as long as possible by building strong foundations that promise continuity. We continue to believe that the perpetuation of our enterprises is a sign of our own progress and development.

As we can see from all the triumphs of human endeavor that we find everywhere around us, humanity has never stopped pursuing new ways to express our pure desire for the eternal, and this has been the catalyst of all our great feats and achievements.

In the final analysis, this constant, abiding pursuit of the eternal is essential to human success. The reason that we have never been able to relinquish the constant desire to attain eternity lies, in essence, in eternity's unattainable nature. We wish to grasp and fathom the world beyond human comprehension, the universe beyond our mortal reach, because we know that we can never fully achieve it, and its elusiveness is where we find its eternal worth. That is why nothing can ever compare to its fathomless value. This is why I know that in moments when we sense the eternal, success is just within our reach.

We know now that a truly successful life comes from pursuing what attracts us, cultivating a heart that is blithe and breezy and full of love, and maintaining a sense of the eternal. But what exactly is success? I describe success in these words:

Success is eternal growth.
Success is eternal progress.
Success issues from eternal passion.
Success arises from eternal courage.
Success arises from eternal effort.
Success creates eternal value.

The Journey to Success

Whenever I am deep in thought about the topic of success, I always remember this story:

Once upon a time, in a faraway land, a poor traveler was journeying in search of work. One day, he arrived in a small, idyllic town, where he told everyone he met, "I came here in search of a career that will make me a successful man. Is there an outstanding job in this town that will help me become successful?" He spoke to as many people as he could find, but everyone he approached gave him the same answer. They all responded, "I'm not sure I understand exactly what you mean by success. All of us here in this town lead very simple lives. We get up at sunrise every morning and go right to our fields, where we spend the entire day working. Our job is to till the fields, water the soil, and feed our crops. Then, when the sun begins to set, we return to our homes to have dinner and spend time with our family. And, finally, we all retire to our beds to sleep. This is how we've all lived for generations. That is why we have never considered looking for a job that will make us successful and why we have never thought about what it means to achieve success. Can you tell us what you mean by a job that is outstanding or that will make you successful?"

The poor traveler answered, "To be successful means to be so accomplished in your career that your achievements draw the envy and acclaim of those around you." The townspeople discussed the traveler's entreaty for help. When they finished, they responded, "You probably won't be able to find exactly what you're looking for here. But there is a town beyond those mountains that some of us have heard of where you may be able to find the kind of success you're searching for."

So the traveler set out from this pastoral village to find this town of the successful beyond the mountains. His journey was long and daunting. During the day, he suffered from hunger pangs and scorching heat. At night, the bitter cold and the echoing howls of wild animals disturbed his sleep.

But he kept walking. He crossed the rivers, climbed the mountains, and scaled the peaks until he finally arrived at his destination. When he reached the town of the successful, he could not contain his joy. This town looked modern and absolutely magnificent. He felt sure that here, he would find the success he so strongly desired.

He asked the townspeople at the gate if they would introduce him to the person in charge of their town. They brought him to their mayor. The mayor appeared to indeed be the picture of wealth and success. He was a plump, impressive man who wore an elegant mustache and refined garments.

When the traveler sat down in front of the mayor, the mayor spent a moment studying him and then began to speak, with a glint in his eyes. "Sir," he said, "as you may already be aware, our town is a community of the successful. Only those who have achieved success are permitted to join this town. From what I can see, however, not only are your clothes in shreds, but you are also penniless and suffering from complete exhaustion. You are clearly in utter shambles. I am sorry to tell you this, but I cannot accept you into our town."

The traveler, feeling somewhat taken aback, objected, "Mayor, please reconsider your decision. I came to your town because I would like to be successful here. Should it really matter whether I am successful right now? Shouldn't it matter more that I will be successful in the future?"

The mayor, again flashing a glint in his eyes, looked into the eyes of the traveler and answered, "If you could look in a mirror, you would see that you have not changed into fresh clothes, eaten any food, or taken any rest. Let me ask you, sir, to consider an important question. Do you believe that success is something that can be achieved overnight? Before you started your journey through the mountains, you should have found a village of people who lead very happy lives. When you met these villagers, didn't you discover anything different about them that you could have learned from? Tell me, what went through your mind when you were spending time with these happy villagers?"

The traveler responded, "I did discover that the people of that village are, indeed, leading very happy lives. But I also found that they showed no particular regard for success. This was the reason I continued my journey in search of this town of the successful. I traveled through many formidable mountains to reach this town. I hope that you and your town will accept me into your community."

When the traveler finished his explanation, the mayor responded, "If that is the case, I would like you to listen to me carefully. To begin with, I need to explain to you that those who are successful, by their nature, are eager to be friends with other accomplished men and women who are more successful than they are. On the other hand, it is in their nature to stay away from people who are likely to bring them misfortune and poverty."

The mayor continued, "You have clearly been mistaken in your idea of success. To become a member of our town, the first step you should have taken was to use the opportunity in the village to start a better, more affluent life. We would have welcomed you, no doubt, if you had made the effort to work and earn enough to buy yourself proper clothing, restore your health, and arrive in the most excellent condition possible. But you didn't do this. You ignored the basic efforts that are expected of all human beings."

"None of us in this town have ever met instant success. To believe in such a thing is to believe that the mountains you crossed could be scaled in a single day. Your first aim should have been to build a happy, affluent life in the village. By doing so, you would have eventually amassed the means to journey on to greater success. But since you neglected to do this, you are not eligible to join our community."

The moral of this story is that we should begin our journey from within our present circumstances and start building successes that are within our grasp. Only after we have achieved this basic success will we truly be ready for greater success. We may dream of suddenly striking it rich and be tempted to look for a way to attain success overnight. But if, for example, our family is in a state of despair, if we are forgetting to cultivate ourselves, or if we lack passion in our work, then we will probably face the same fate as the poor traveler's: the world of the successful won't accept us no matter how many mountains and rivers we cross to reach it.

Each time I remember this story, I feel impassioned to tell as many people as possible that the successful are always eager to befriend those who are also successful and are weary of associating with those who are not. I sincerely hope that you will take heed of this wisdom as I have throughout my life, and always keep it close to your heart on your journey to success.

TWO

The Conditions of Successful Living

Joy of the Soul

In this chapter, I would like to discuss the three conditions for attaining success: cultivating nobility, confidence, and courage. But before I begin, there is a premise to all of these conditions that is so essential that success is impossible without it. That premise is to feel the joy of the soul.

What do I mean by "the joy of the soul"? The joy of the soul is the sheer delight that issues from deep within our hearts. At times, it is also the profound pleasure that may move us to tremor with pure delight. I wonder how many people in this world have had the opportunity to experience this joy. I can't help but notice that many people in this modern age seem to be going through life without ever truly knowing spiritual joy.

Many of us, nowadays, are attracted to forms of entertainment such as watching movies, going to theaters, and attending sports events. The amusement that these activities offer is a shallow level of joy, but we have come to depend on them as our only source of excitement—our only way to feel emotionally moved or touched. That may feel natural to people who have never encountered spiritual joy; perhaps this is the only joy that they can imagine life bringing.

But once you have experienced the joy of the soul, the excitement and exhilaration of these activities pale in comparison. These leisure activities feel fleeting and insubstantial, and you realize that to go through life chasing this sort of happiness means choosing a life without true meaningfulness.

Where do we find true spiritual joy? Reading a good book that leaves a powerful impact on us is one way. This kind of book imparts an abiding happiness that will always remain with us. I have read many books in my life, some of which gave me so much inspiration and pleasure that the previous books that used to inspire me inevitably lost their spell. Encounters with such books can be truly life changing. A good book leaves an impact so remarkable that it feels as if our soul has been swept away.

I remember when I first became passionate for books about the human heart and mind. I devoured as many works as I could possibly lay my hands on, one after another, and kept going as if it were never enough. I pored over each one intensely. But even then, it was only once in a blue moon that I chanced upon one that truly satisfied my soul.

Books like these were so scarce that I randomly chose books by the hundreds and perused each of them to find the one jewel. As forlorn as this process felt, I didn't want to give up, because these books do exist, and I believed that I would find them as long as I kept searching.

I even extended my search to widely acclaimed foreign authors. But to my dismay, many of these works did not touch my soul the way I had expected them to. I tried to determine whether something had been lost in translation or whether there was some other reason for it.

In a sense, I found that I simply wanted to know more about

the mind than the author had delved into. I wanted to find out more about what remained to be discovered. And I believed that when I did, what I found would be a treasure that would nourish our hearts and souls, foster our spiritual growth, and benefit our lives in this world. With this inner conviction, I read extensively, opening every book I could possibly find.

But then, one day, I realized something that made me finally end my search. I decided to end my constant quest for works by other authors. Instead of searching in vain for books by someone else, I determined that I would write them myself.

I realized that if I could no longer find books that brought me true fulfillment, then I could be the one to write such books. I could choose to become an author and create nourishing books that I would want to read, time and time again. I thought that perhaps there was such a thing as writing your own books to relish throughout your life. And that in doing so, I would also be able to offer these books to all those who were seeking the same spiritual happiness that I was.

The passion that stirred me then continues to abide within me to this day, as I continue to write books. Ever since the day of my epiphany, I have written prolifically. I have published book after book, year after year. In the United States these days, over three hundred thousand new titles are published each year. That may sound like plenty of books to offer eager readers. But I know from personal experience that even three hundred thousand books do not guarantee one that will be spiritually fulfilling.

I wish that I didn't understand this sense of frustration as keenly as I do. But if you have experienced true joy of the soul before, you can probably relate to my story. Books that offer spiritual joy are as difficult to find as a needle in a haystack. So I am certain that many people experience the same dilemma today.

As my journey to my career as an author illustrates, we attain true spiritual joy when we put our heart and soul into our work and persevere until we have successfully brought work of true value and delight to others. By bringing spiritual joy to as many people as possible, I am rewarded with my own spiritual joy and success every day. Pursuing my own spiritual joy led me to find it by serving this need in others. We human beings experience sheer delight when we can truly believe in and be proud of the work we have accomplished.

I feel more and more joy every time I am able to bring nourishment to another person's heart. This shows that my soul now aspires to an even higher degree of joy. It shows, too, that our spiritual joy grows twofold, threefold, or even fourfold when we draw our own happiness from bringing happiness to others.

An Aura of Nobility

The first condition for attaining success is to cultivate an air of nobility. Nobility is a quality of human character that books on success seldom discuss. But imagine your first impression of a person acting suspiciously or appearing famished. It's unlikely that your first impression was of a successful person, even though the person you were imagining might actually own tremendous wealth. The same idea can apply to someone with the opposite appearance: even if you meet a person with a portly physique, if he behaves crudely, you probably won't perceive him as a successful person. We get these impressions of these people because we naturally expect those who are successful to be dignified and noble.

As you can see, unless your nobility develops in concert with your success, your success will appear inauthentic. Truly successful people emanate a soft aura of divine dignity and nobility.

A simple way to tell whether you are advancing toward success and accumulating genuine achievement is to look into the mirror every day. Although you may not realize it, your face is a reflection of the changes that occur within your character. Each day, your soul's experiences are leaving their marks behind in the same way that each year, a new ring is engraved in a tree trunk.

The marks of nobility may not show up immediately or even in six months or a year, but as three years, five years, and ten years go by, these marks will steadily become recognizable to yourself and others. Eventually, others should be able to perceive your nobility simply by being in your presence.

If, on the other hand, you cannot distinguish an air of nobility in your features even after ten years of continued success, then you may need to reconsider the intentions that have motivated your successes.

There are forms of success that result in external outcomes such as wealth, prestige, status, and recognition, but to represent authentic success, these outcomes need to be accompanied by a noble character. What this essentially means is that true success cultivates our spirituality. If this idea is unfamiliar, it basically means that success improves our character. This means that our success is only authentic if it enhances our personal character.

So how do we cultivate a noble character? There are three essential ways to do so.

The first is to develop our perceptive abilities. To cultivate both character and success, we need to be able to counsel a diverse range of people and offer solutions to their problems. We also need to be able to resolve our own problems and personal dilemmas.

The second way to cultivate a noble character is to nurture the kind of quiet strength of character that influences people. This quality is beautifully illustrated by a Chinese proverb: "The peach tree gathers people purely by being still and silent." People are naturally drawn to the foot of a peach tree even though it stands silently, because they are attracted by its delicious fruits and beautiful flowers. In the same way, people gather to a person of nobility because they are attracted by the influence of the person's character. When your character is enhanced by nobility, you will see the proof in the people who are drawn to you.

I believe this proverb to be very true. As we develop nobility of character, our natural influence over others grows along with it. We can all use our words and actions to try to influence people, but those of truly noble character influence others through their whole way of being. The people around them are naturally affected by their character as it shines through their bearing and deportment. So the more noble your character becomes, the more you'll find yourself having a natural influence over those around you. Your overall air and the atmosphere you create will naturally inspire others to pursue their own self-development.

In this sense, true educators do not rely on words or actions. They depend on the influence of their character as it emanates through their presence. They exude a spiritual atmosphere that inspires the people around them to develop their own virtue and to pursue their own self-development.

The third way to cultivate a noble character is to become more tolerant and generous. On one hand, nobility of character enables us to perceive people's thoughts, emotions, and problems. This perceptiveness is valuable, but when we develop it too far, we start to notice people's faults, mistakes, and wrongdoings more keenly, and we begin to pass judgment on people and label them as good or bad and capable or incompetent.

When someone who is acknowledged for a noble and high-minded character leaves an impression of narrow-mindedness, in most cases, it is because this person is being judgmental. In cultivating nobility, we become sensitive to the indecencies, faults, and undesirable habits that are bound to exist in others. But if we become judgmental and critical, we risk exchanging some of our noble-mindedness for intolerance. This is why it is important to cultivate open-mindedness in concert with nobility and to ground both in a heart of tolerance.

To be tolerant is to look upon others with a heart of love that embraces them with acceptance. Tolerance allows us to accept all people for who they are because it changes the way we perceive them. Instead of seeing them narrowly, in terms of their relative, one-on-one relationship with us, we come to see them from an open-minded perspective based on wholehearted compassion. This is the hallmark of tolerance.

To practice tolerance, we need a foundation of careful introspection. An eye of tolerance can't be built without a deep understanding of the faults and weaknesses of our own human condition. Being fully aware of our own imperfections allows us to recognize that we are being forgiven and fostered by all those who know us, regardless of our flaws. This realization grows into gratitude, and this gratitude grows into a heart of compassion and tolerance toward everyone as sharing the same human condition as ourselves.

These three conditions of nobility—perceptiveness, an influential character, and tolerance—are essential hallmarks of true success.

The Confidence to Succeed

The second condition for attaining success is to have confidence. If we look around us, we see that some people fail repeatedly and that these people share a particular pattern of mind: a tendency to desire failure.

The desire to fail is basically the same as the desire for unhappiness. When we seek unhappiness, we live each day as if we were constantly looking for the seeds of misery. We always manage to find something to be unhappy about, either in something someone else said to us or within our circumstances. For example, some people are always seeing people's faults and mistakes at work, and others are always pointing out their spouse's flaws. This is a universal human pattern that we see all over the world and throughout history.

What these people all share is a subconscious urge to plunge themselves into a state of misery. They don't realize it, but they're indulging a self-destructive, self-defeating impulse.

Why do they subconsciously desire self-destruction and unhappiness, when it should be a basic human wish to succeed and be happy? There are two possible reasons. The first is a deep sense of guilt or shame, and the second is accumulated, pent-up discontent and dissatisfaction. Both of these are states of mind that lead to unhappiness.

If you feel shackled by guilt or shame, consider whether the values behind these feelings are really valid. For example, some people who repeatedly fail and who have a religious personality admit that they loathe the idea of financial prosperity. If you have a similar aversion to prosperity, you are choosing values that allow success to escape you. A part of you inside is deliberately rejecting prospects that look promising, and this is obviously going to make it difficult for you to attract wealth and success.

The same pattern holds for people who struggle with guilt and shame in their romantic relationships. When people keep running into problems in their romantic relationships, those problems are most often a manifestation of their guilt and subconscious, self-destructive impulses.

I wish I could go up to everyone who has a lot of dissatisfaction built up inside and tell them that they need to make a clear choice between happiness and unhappiness. If their choice is to be unhappy, then any help that is offered them will be in vain. Even God cannot save them if unhappiness is what they desire.

Happiness begins with making a decision to be happy. You will find happiness when you decide that happiness is what you want.

Many people aren't aware of this. Many of us go through life unmindfully and inadvertently making choices that make us unhappy. For example, do you tend to brood about how unhappy you are? When you stop to consider it, do you spend most of your time mulling over how miserable you are? Do you enact stories in your mind about unhappy endings in your life?

If you do any of these things, you should consider going

back to the starting point and deciding whether your desire is to be happy or not to be happy. That is the real question.

If your decision is to be unhappy, then you need to take responsibility for this decision regardless of the miseries you will face in life. Because it is a choice you made yourself, you will need to hold yourself accountable and keep your discontents and dissatisfactions to yourself, because talking about them can give others unpleasant feelings.

If, on the contrary, your decision is to be happy, then you will need to firmly resolve to attain happiness. The strong determination you put into your decision will give you confidence and allow you to keep going. As you face society's notions of "cannots" and "should nots" and preconceived ideas about right and wrong, you must stand firm against these pressures and ask yourself, "Is there anything really wrong with seeking happiness and working to pave a path to a happier future?"

People sometimes criticize and obstruct the work of those who appear weak, as if to throw rocks at them. But there is truth in the Chinese proverb, "When you act with all your resolve, even demons will keep out of your way." The confidence in our heart has the power to move their hearts. When we move forward with resolute self-confidence, even evil will hesitate to obstruct our path.

In addition, our confidence attracts other confident people to us. In chapter one, I shared with you a story about a town of the successful. Just as the people of this town attracted other successful people because they were successful themselves, if you want to become friends with successful people, you will need to first become successful yourself.

People who have attained success have been able to do so because they have maintained the distinct energy of success in their minds, and this energy has emanated an atmosphere of success around them. This aura keeps away people who have a tendency to fail and attracts those who succeed. So if you have a history of failure, you won't have much luck trying to associate with the successful in the hope of benefiting from their success.

Even if you happen on success by pure luck, this kind of success is fleeting and will eventually vanish because it didn't come from the confidence in your mind. Confidence is the driving force that the successful draw on to create this aura of success. I cannot emphasize enough how important it is to stop brooding over your unhappiness and instead decide whether you want to be happy or unhappy. If your true desire is to be happy, then say it to yourself out loud. Make up your mind to be happy. Because when you do, you will see the next thing that you must do: be confident that you will find your happiness.

Feel the strength of the confidence inside you. Use this confidence to become successful in the world of your mind, in the world of your thoughts.

When you create the image of success in the world of your mind, everything that you need will come to you. Friends and associates who have attained success will surround you. And you will begin to emanate your own aura of success. You will attract all these things to you as if you had a magnetic force. Only if you have the confidence to harness their blessings will you be graced with the presence of the goddesses of victory, success, and happiness.

In Times of Despair, Set Simple Goals

Have you ever been struck by a setback so disheartening that you could no longer see the way forward? Have you been driven to such exhaustion that your mind seemed to stop working? Are you facing a life crisis that is plunging you into despair? There are times in life when we run into adversities that make us feel so defeated that we lose all enthusiasm to keep going.

What can we do to lift ourselves out of such despair and rediscover the world of wonder? We can take one basic step, and that is simply to set a goal for ourselves. When we are stuck in a pit of despair, setting a goal is like throwing a rope up to the surface, catching a rock, and using the unmoving solidity of the rock to pull ourselves out. It's even better if we can attach an ice pick to the rope and have it catch the root of a tree.

If you are currently feeling disheartened, despondent, and anguished, this is what you can do to help yourself: just as you might throw up a rope to climb out of a pit, you can set new life goals to help you climb out of the pit of despair.

To start with, get two sheets of paper. On the first sheet, write down your goals in life, dividing them into big goals, medium goals, and small goals. On the second sheet, list when you want to aim to accomplish each goal: immediately, in the near future, and in the longer term. You now have two plans that will be vital in lifting yourself out of the pit.

When you are finished setting these goals, begin working on the most manageable ones that you can start right away. Begin applying yourself to your small goals that you can get to immediately. This should help you determine specifically what you will do to pull yourself out of despair.

As you find your way out of the pit, you have a choice between two different ropes or paths. One rope will take you on a completely new journey. With this rope, you will be taking a path you have never traveled before and have never imagined taking. The second rope will lead you to a path that you can take to start over from the beginning.

The key is to set a goal of persevering for a specific amount of time. For example, if you have hit rock bottom, then just getting through today may be the best goal you can set yourself. If you are faring a little better than that, you could look into the near future and try to pull through until the end of the week.

Then, when you have reached these goals, you can keep setting longer spans of time. You can aim to hold out one more month, then three more months, then six more months, and then a year. The passage of time as you keep going in this manner will help you weather this period of distress in your life. Time is on our side when we're making an effort, and time will open a path to those who persevere.

When you are deciding which path to take, there is something important that you should consider. If the source of your distress or sense of failure lies in problems in your relationships, that is a circumstance that you can definitely change and improve. Acts of nature, such as natural disasters, are beyond human control. But the crises we face in our relationships are well within our power to resolve over time.

I have had my share of these experiences, and what they have taught me is that these periods of despair do not last longer than a year. My most difficult period did not last longer than six months.

By giving yourself a chance to persevere and improve your circumstances, you will notice your anguish subsiding, and you will feel new light being breathed into you. Perhaps you were tempted to believe that everything around you was meant to hurt you. But over time, you will see that there are also people around you that are casting their light of kindness and support upon you. Your decision to believe these things to be true and your perseverance are sure to help you in times of despair.

The Courage to Move Forward

If we have courage, nothing is impossible. That is why living each day as bravely as we can is the third and final essential condition to attaining success in life.

The first time we fail at an endeavor, we understand that we need to have courage and pull ourselves back up. But when we fail a second time and yet a third time, we may begin to feel as though there can't possibly be any more courage left inside us. We can endure failure only so many times before we begin to anticipate only a series of further catastrophes. We humans are capable of valorous acts of courage in rare moments of crisis. But when a prolonged period of adversity, a time of hardship, or an age of crisis is brought upon us, it can be a daunting task to continue to live fearlessly every day. This is when we begin to look backwards in search of a way out of situations.

We shouldn't get caught up in assuming that every circumstance lying ahead of us will be detrimental. Also in front of us are opportunities that will allow us to create a path to success. Unless we decide to be brave and go forward, we may not even be able to find these opportunities, let alone seize them.

Have you ever gone fishing for crawfish before? If you have ever tried to catch one, you will know how easy it is to do. Crawfish are freshwater crustaceans that look like small lobsters and typically live in rivers and streams. To catch them, all you need to know is that they swim backwards about seven to ten inches the moment that they sense danger. They can be easily frightened by the sound of a footstep, the splash of a fish, or the drop of a stone. So all you need to do to catch them is drop a stone in front of them while holding a net seven to ten inches behind them. Because swimming backwards is their only defensive maneuver, once they are caught in the net, they don't know how to escape. I used to go fishing for crawfish frequently as a child, so I know from direct experience that this method works every time.

Just as these crawfish don't realize that peril can be lurking behind them, not just in front of them, people who only look backwards for an escape route to safety will end up trapped by a calamity hovering behind them. In the end, retreating from challenging circumstances won't truly save us from adverse situations. Having the courage to take action and move forward instead of backward is the real way to save ourselves and move toward success.

If we are struggling with repeated mistakes, failures, or setbacks, we are probably feeling indecisive and are at a loss about what to do. This is why we become slow to take action. We also are trying to avoid taking risks and want to prevent further circumstances, situations, and contact with others from adding to our existing fear, anguish, and pain. This is why we keep searching behind us for a way to escape.

If you find yourself in this predicament, consider in which direction you would rather face adversity when it comes to knock you down. If the possibility of failure could be behind you as much as it could be in front of you, then wouldn't it be more worthwhile to collapse courageously facing forward instead of backward? Wouldn't you feel more pride and honor in yourself this way? Which of these ways of life would you rather be remembered for when you are gone from this world?

When you decide to have courage and to take action, you won't ever truly fail in what you do, no matter what the results may turn out to be. This is why decision and action are two important elements of living with courage and attaining success in life.

Courage requires decision and action. Courage is not something given to you; it is something that arises from within when you decide to prevail over fear. From the moment you make this decision and begin to move forward again, your courage will rise and will keep rising, time and again. I promise you that you will be astonished by the inner reserves of strength and courage that have been within you all along.

THREE

The Secrets of Successful Living

Keeping a Cheerful Attitude

Maintaining a cheerful attitude as we move through life is the first secret to successful living. Simply put, living a successful life means living with an ongoing sense of cheer. But we often ascribe conditions to our notions of success that wind up keeping us from being cheerful. How often have you thought, "I would be happy *if only* I had this," "I will be happy *if only* these conditions are satisfied," or "I would be happy *if only* my circumstances change in the specific ways I want them to"?

Let me urge you to rid yourself of such thoughts, for these notions may drown you in mediocrity. Cheerfulness is always an option, no matter what our circumstances are—no matter where we are or what conditions we face, and even when situations are against us.

As a matter of fact, we can say that a cheerful disposition proves to be truly extraordinary when it prevails through times of crisis and adversity. It is not very difficult to live cheerfully when your heart is wholly blissful and when your life is at the peak of happiness. But when you are burdened by inopportune circumstances, harrowed by grief, or afflicted by hardship, can you continue to preserve a state of cheer? This is our true test.

Life brings sunny days, but it is also sure to bring storms that may, at times, go on for as long as a year. And as we know, dark clouds can create miserable conditions—cold temperatures, harsh winds, and torrential rain. But even so, the sun continues to shine radiantly above the clouds. No matter how dense the darkness may appear, we must not fall into believing that it is the real state of this world, and we must not anticipate desperate circumstances to come. Instead, we should believe in the brightness of the sunshine beyond the clouds.

All we need to do to find the brightness again is break through the black clouds. But how do we do this?

First, before we do anything else, we need to resolve to stay cheerful, regardless of the circumstances. The first step is to make the choice and put in the effort to maintain a cheerful and blithe attitude. We are blessed with infinite reserves of determination, so we can learn to draw on our reserves in times of severe hardship, even when we feel as though we're at the end of our rope. When we firmly determine to muster a cheerful attitude in spite of challenging circumstances, life will, from time to time, open a new path forward.

If you are thinking thoughts of defeat, I urge you to hold on a while longer. Consider it this way: defeat is a choice that is open to you at any time, and surrendering to it doesn't require any special ability. Anyone is capable of giving in. It is easy to settle for defeat, especially when you are feeling discouraged.

It is how cheerfully we prevail through these trials that determines our success in life. Life brings these times of hardship indiscriminately to us all as opportunities to strengthen our souls.

These seemingly insurmountable conditions are an opportunity to make use of our reserves of determination so we can endure for another six months or year.

Our aim in life, therefore, is not to be cheerful only when we are recognized for our accomplishments. Rather, our aim is to take advantage of these times of insuperable odds as our best opportunities to live with a carefree, graceful, and cheerful heart, as if we were galloping upon a white stallion and dashing gallantly through enemy ranks.

We do have the potential to live this way. This capacity to be strong—expressly because we are in the face of crisis—is, without doubt, inside us all.

This is something I am always mindful of. When a fair breeze begins to blow, I focus intensely on my work. Then, when the winds turn against me, I strengthen my defenses and persevere. I keep moving forward. It is as though, when we keep moving forward regardless of what besets us, we give life no choice but to open up paths to opportunity and achievement.

When you are feeling discouraged and your spirits are low, simply take a look into a mirror and determine whether other people would want to lend their help, support, and guidance to someone with a countenance like yours. You will realize that they probably wouldn't. On the other hand, they would probably be delighted to offer their assistance to someone who is persevering with strong determination. So I urge you to put on your smile and move forward with renewed spirit.

Offering the Gift of a Smile

How, then, can we live cheerfully? What can we do to maintain a cheerful attitude around others on a day-to-day basis? Some of us may feel so low that we do not know what to do to be cheerful again.

The first thing to begin with is simply to wear a cheerful smile. No matter how difficult our circumstances may be, we are always capable of smiling. And by smiling, we spread our cheer to everyone we see throughout our day. When we realize that our smile has delighted someone, it doubles the joy in our own heart.

So at the end of each day, look back and consider the following questions: How often did you offer your smile to the people you encountered over the course of your day? How long were you able to smile, even when no one else was around?

These questions should bring to your attention that there is a principle at the basis of a smile. This principle says that our smiles are proportional to the effort we put into them. We tend to believe that people who have a beautiful smile must have been naturally born with it. We assume that, when someone is able to smile continuously, good things must be happening to her all the time. But the truth is most likely very different.

Her troubles may only remain unseen. No one, not even someone who smiles all the time, is completely immune to life's griefs and hardships. All of us are subject to circumstances that threaten to turn our smiles into frowns or to fill our faces with deep wrinkles of anxiety. Those who keep smiling in spite of life's challenges do so through persistent perseverance, and what they accomplish is a truly extraordinary feat.

On the other hand, if there actually existed a person who never had to face an ounce of misfortune, then this person would also have lived a remarkable life. This is because pessimistic thoughts tend to attract further negative thoughts to our mind. For example, a habit of pessimistic thinking can make us believe that the lightest footsteps belong to thieves, that a hint of misfortune is an omen of calamity, or that the sniffles are a sign of a fatal illness. So if you live your entire life without any hardship, it means that you were able to keep your mind clear of any negative thoughts that could have attracted misfortune to you. This, in itself, is an extraordinary accomplishment. It shows that you were truly loved by God.

As you can see, no matter how we get there, our ability to smile absolutely depends on the effort we put into it. There is always perseverance behind a smile that pretense alone can't bring us. No matter who we are, if we live with a smile, it means we are making an effort to do so.

So the vital question of our life is, how long can we keep our smile? This is not too difficult to do during our thirties, but it becomes harder as we grow into our forties, fifties, and sixties. For this reason, our smile is an essential form of spiritual training. As we continue to smile, we are disciplining our mind to handle our troubles cheerfully. By making this effort, we reap a precious reward: the smile that will decorate our faces in the other world, once we've finished our time in this world.

The effort to smile is important to our lives because the world becomes a better place with each additional person that is able to smile. A smile is a compassionate act of giving like the beauty of a flower on the side of the road. It may only rarely attract our notice, but if, for a split second, we become captivated by its beauty as we walk past it, then this flower has given us its compassion and altruism. Most people never give a thought to the purpose of this flower. Yet, it continues to show its beautiful blossoms to delight as many people as possible.

While the sight of a withering flower gives us a sense of sadness, a flower in the peak of bloom reminds us of a beautiful, beaming smile. When we set our eyes upon a garden in springtime, all the blooms appear like a crowd of smiles gleaming in our direction. In this way, the flowers of this world teach us that even they have found their way of offering their compassionate smiles to the world.

Animals contribute wonderful smiles to the world, too. Dogs are strikingly capable of showing us their most cheerful smiles. Some people say that dogs are not capable of showing their feelings, but this is not true. If you have ever owned a pet dog, you know how adeptly they convey their emotions of sadness, anger, and joy. I don't know anyone who has come home to their joyous dog and not been delighted by how happily it welcomes them home. So it is with us humans and our relationships with other people: as long as we approach others with a smile, it is very difficult for them not to feel delighted by it.

If even flowers and dogs can make the effort to show us their beautiful smiles, then it would be a shame if we human beings were not able to make a greater effort to offer our smiles to the world.

As you can now see, one of the secrets to living cheerfully throughout life is to keep smiling, no matter what befalls us, and to keep making an effort to do so even when times are rough. By doing so, we contribute precious joy to others and help make this world a better place for all.

Making Use of Positive Words

Successful living requires more than wearing a smile; we also need to consider the words we speak. We humans, by our nature, are prone to speaking negatively during bouts of grief and distress. Dark times are apt to get the better of us, and dark words unwittingly slip from our lips.

We need to make a conscious effort to tame our words to prevent ourselves from becoming trapped in a loop. Just as a smile adorns our face, the words we speak adorn our character. The thoughts that we frequently voice create the atmosphere that emanates from our presence. When the majority of what we say is negative, people sense that associating with us could make them unhappy, and this drives them away from us. This can then become a negative loop: as more people begin to keep their distance from us, we become more prone to becoming pessimistic and vocally negative, which only adds to the unpleasant atmosphere that hangs around us.

When we fall into this negative cycle, the key to getting out of it is to take the unhappy aspects of life with a grain of salt while exaggerating the happy aspects. To do this, we avoid voicing discontent and dissatisfaction, even if we are in the midst of distress.

All of us have the occasional morning when we run into trouble just as we are about to leave the house. If we handle it by dwelling on negative feelings and talking about it all day, we'll have a negative impact not only on our own life but also on the lives of those around us. Alternatively, we have the choice to talk about something fantastic that happened instead of what went wrong. In fact, periods of distress are the perfect time to discover and talk about the happy and fortunate aspects of life. This not only lifts our own spirits, but also delights those who associate with us.

A second problem with speaking negatively is that as we do so, our negative thoughts become ever more deeply impressed upon our minds. And these negative effects are not limited to ourselves: our words also leave their imprint on the minds of those around us. When we verbalize our negative thoughts, we release them into the world as a form of floating energy that drifts and travels all over the world. This energy can leave a dark wound in people's hearts like the mark made by the claws of a crow.

All these consequences explain why it is essential that we abandon negative speech as much as we can. Underlying these reasons is an even deeper one: we must abandon negative speech out of love for others and ourselves. If you truly cherish, value, and want to take care of yourself, you will not wish to blemish your heart with negative or pessimistic words, especially in times of grief and adversity. Rather, you should speak with strong words of positive and constructive energy to expel those dark emotions of the heart.

This is one of the most essential methods of successful living. Successful people persistently speak positively and constructively. They say things that brighten everyone's hearts.

We might say that our words resemble tow trucks or horse carriages. Just as the horses pull the carriage forward, the words we speak harness tremendous power to pull our lives ahead.

While positive words are capable of pulling us forward, negative words are apt to pull us backward. In the latter case, we never manage to get to our destination, no matter how far we travel. But we can choose to use our words to our advantage by adding positive horsepower to our carriage. We can add one horse to our carriage by saying one positive thing. Then, by saying a second positive thing, we can add yet another horse, and so on. We can keep increasing our horsepower by making use of positive words.

So if you succeed at saying one positive thing, you can commend yourself for strengthening your power. By strengthening your power, you will increase your speed. Not only that—you'll also be able to carry a greater number of people and a larger load of cargo to a positive destination.

In the final analysis, the words we choose to speak determine our happiness or unhappiness, and this is why controlling our words is another secret to successful and positive living.

Seeing the Positive in Every Situation

The next secret to successful living in the midst of hardship is to consider the situation from the opposite standpoint. What I mean is that we need to see the bright side of our circumstances. We can always find a positive meaning hidden within every roadblock, obstruction, or failure.

For example, suppose you are a student who has just discovered that you weren't accepted into any of your prospective colleges. This would come as a terrible shock to anyone. You may feel deeply hurt and rejected. If you were to react pessimistically to this situation, your first thought might be, "This just goes to show that I am not intelligent enough. What will I do if I can't improve my score on the SAT next year? I have already gotten off on the wrong foot for the bright future that was supposed to lie ahead of me."

However, if you stop yourself there and look at the situation from the opposite point of view, you'll discover that this situation can have a positive purpose in your life. There are several possible perspectives you can consider.

The first perspective says, "This could be a way for God to give me a chance to attend an even better college. Studying for another year might help me get accepted into an even better college than I would have been able to otherwise. Maybe this is the real meaning of these colleges' rejections."

The second perspective says, "This must be an ordeal that

can teach me how to handle hardships in life and enrich me with meaningful experience. What I learn from this experience will probably become the wisdom I draw on when I am in a position to guide others in the future. This is my opportunity to learn about how to persevere through hardships in life. I am thankful for this chance to cultivate the inner strength that will prepare me to achieve great things."

A third point of view says, "Perhaps this ordeal is God's way of showing me that I have been too full of myself until now. This must be an experience designed to teach me the value of humility. Perhaps now is the time in my life when I will have the chance to reflect on myself with real humility so I can grasp the true value of diligence and effort. From this point on, I will stop seeking recognition from others and instead will make it my purpose in life to accomplish something truly meaningful. Now is my chance to start life over again with deeper humility and work steadily to build up my abilities over time. This must be the meaning of my failure."

There are even more takeaways that I can think of. Another way to come at this situation is to say, "Perhaps the things I do while I'm waiting to be accepted somewhere will become the basis of a novel when I am a famous writer. Many famous writers draw inspiration from their lives, so perhaps this is the way that life works—we transform experiences like this into great works of literature."

Perhaps you can also think of it this way: "I have heard that the friendships we create during this difficult time of life often become lifelong friendships because of the trust and support we give each other. Perhaps this year will bring me meaningful friendships that will last forever. Maybe this is my chance to meet true kindred spirits."

Or you can also take it this way: "If this sets me back an entire year, that just means that I'll have to live a little longer than I'd planned. Instead of living until I'm eighty, now I will just have to live until I'm eighty-one. I'll use the time that I now have before I begin college to build my physical strength and take care of my health to prepare for longevity."

Many successful businesspeople faced ordeals and hardships at a relatively young age. The experiences of their youth helped them cultivate true strength of the soul. I believe that a life without hardship is not necessarily better for you in terms of your spiritual growth. Life sometimes confronts us with ordeals and setbacks that threaten to hold us down, and I believe that when we can cultivate the inner strength and perseverance to overcome these hardships, it helps bring out the true sparkle of our soul.

This applies to not only young people, but also the middle-aged and the elderly. For example, if you are now in your sixties and are reaching retirement, you may be thinking that there is nothing more that you can accomplish. If you still had the vitality of your youthful days, clearly, you'd be full of possibilities. But you may feel that there is nothing else that you can possibly do at such a late stage in life.

But I believe that reverse thinking can be used even in this scenario to make better choices that strengthen your soul. It is a matter of shifting your perspective to recognize the possibility of turning your retirement into a second youth. There is nothing impossible about this idea. All you really need is the burn of youthful ambition in your heart. When you awaken the power of your dreams, the vitality to achieve the things you'd want to do if you were decades younger will emerge of its own volition. Our true physical age loses all significance in the face of our determination to keep reaching for new goals and high aspirations.

The same holds true for anyone going through a demotion or setback at work. Many mid-level executives face this kind of hardship, and it can be an especially trying time in the course of one's life. But if we look at this situation from a positive standpoint, we may see that our circumstances are offering us the perfect environment for developing inner strength. If you are demoted to a less intense position, you can use it as an opportunity to rejuvenate your strength and apply yourself to self-cultivation. The same holds true even if you are moved to a very busy department. This may be your opportunity to put your very best effort into fulfilling your department's goals.

The key is to find the opportunities within the most desperate of circumstances and use them to blossom into your most beautiful life.

Just as school, work, and retirement play a significant role in the outcome of our lives, so does marriage. Some women, for example, spend a lot of time carefully looking for a partner they feel is truly meant for them and for a relationship in which both partners are meant for each other, but they may find their expectations shattered when they actually get married and see that their marriage is not turning out the way they had imagined it. This kind of thing can also happen in relationships between family members.

When the ideals we hold most dear to our hearts are crumbling before our eyes, we can become very discouraged and susceptible to negative thinking. But if we allow the pain to live on within us, we won't glean the real purpose of our spiritual training in this life. Dealing with our problems by harboring disappointment will actually mean letting go of the purpose of our life.

We mustn't look for fair weather to sail through to avoid a crisis, especially when the problem is part of an important aspect of our lives. Life does indeed expose us to the harsh elements of the sea. There are storms, heavy winds, and torrential rain, and we may need to stop at a harbor for safety or bail seawater out of our ship. There may also be times when the wind snaps our mast in half or tears our sails into shreds.

The most important thing we can do in these circumstances is to stay strong and sail on through the storm. The key to life is to continue to ask ourselves, "What is the best way forward? What is the best decision I can make to allow my soul to shine through?" This is the attitude that gives us the strength to sail through life's tempests.

If you ever feel trapped in the midst of a crisis or a hardship with no way out and no solution in sight, stop and consider how many solutions you have come up with so far in your life. You may believe that there is no way out and that you have come to a dead end, but reconsider whether this is really true. Are you sure that you've exhausted all the possibilities?

Often, there are more possibilities than we realize. We may have crossed these possibilities off because we assumed that they wouldn't be accepted by society, that people would be against them, or that we don't have enough confidence to carry them through. Just because of reasons like these, we are apt to eliminate so many possibilities and limit our solutions.

The key to resolving our problems in life is to keep thinking of as many solutions as possible and keep searching for the one that will help us resolve the issues at hand in the smartest, quickest, and most efficient way. As we keep going, we will eventually amass the wisdom we'll need to help others swiftly resolve the problems in their lives.

Believing in Endless Possibilities

The heart of reverse thinking is realizing that the possibilities are endless. Just imagine the excitement you will feel when adopting this point of view opens an array of possibilities before your eyes.

Adverse circumstances may make us feel like we have no choice—that there is only one way forward. This assumption can throw us into despair if that one path becomes laden with obstacles. But what appears to our eyes as a solitary path may appear to someone else as a web of countless intertwining paths like a checkerboard. In reality, we are always surrounded by many paths to our goal, and these paths will open for us if we just take one step to the left or right. There are many possibilities in reality, and we can forge new paths in any way we'd like.

Some people may criticize this kind of mindset as an example of opportunism or indecisiveness. But they are mistaken in this view. Such claims are not true.

When we humans are imparted with life, we are also granted the liberty of free will. We have the privilege and the responsibility to exercise our free will to make good choices throughout our lives. We should use our free will to the fullest degree to make the best possible decisions for our lives. We need to stop assuming that there's only one way forward, that we have no choice but to follow the path in front of us. Instead, we need to keep searching for all the other possibilities that might lead to even better outcomes.

This mindset of believing in possibilities is also essential to the management of a business. The success of a business is largely determined by how consistently we come up with new ideas and improved methods of accomplishing our work.

This also holds true in our interactions with those around us. The ability to adapt ourselves flexibly to serve others' needs is vital to our success in life. It is not always beneficial to be attached to one solitary way of thinking or one way of handling situations and trying to impose that way on others. There is no escaping that some people will agree with your ideas while others will subscribe to their own points of view. How open we remain to the diversity of ideas in this world has a significant impact on the progress we make in life.

If we imagine ourselves living in a flat, two-dimensional world, a world with limited maneuverability, we will become despondent as soon as we become lost in a maze of problems. The limitations we face in this scenario may only spell doom. But if we can lift our gaze and imagine a three-dimensional world instead, it will be much easier to see all the possible routes out of the maze. There may be no way out of the maze if we limit ourselves to moving two-dimensionally in our flat world, but when we open our minds to the possibility of jumping over walls, as a flea would jump into the air to get from one point to another, the possibilities become endless.

We discover new possibilities when we shift our perspective from a two-dimensional point of view to a three-dimensional standpoint. Similarly, if you are currently grappling with a problem and finding yourself at a standstill, you can discover the solution by approaching it from a different angle. When we lift our heads and see our lives as holding endless possibilities, we can create a life of success.

If fleas are capable of freeing themselves from a maze by looking at it from a third-dimensional point of view, then we humans should be capable of resolving our problems by elevating our point of view to a fourth-dimensional standpoint. Most of us have become accustomed to thinking vertically when we're looking for solutions. For example, if we've been digging into the ground to create a well but we haven't yet found any water, most of us are apt to conclude that we just haven't dug deeply enough. So we keep digging further and further. If we don't find a water spring at fifty meters down, our decision is usually to dig further toward a hundred meters. If that is still not enough, we will keep going down to 150 meters, and then two hundred meters, and so forth. This is what I mean by vertical thinking. This is the most common pattern of thinking that we use to solve our problems.

But we human beings are also capable of lateral thinking. Lateral thinking, in this analogy, means realizing that the underground spring could lie in elsewhere. Instead of digging in a single place, we can consider digging in several places at the same time to improve our chances of success. In real life, these kinds of solutions exist and are open to us, but we don't notice them. In our day-to day lives, we resemble the well digger who believes that digging further in the same location is the only available solution, whereas the real solution lies in digging elsewhere.

The soundness of this perspective is obvious in a visual analogy like this one. But when it comes to the abstract problems of life, it can be hard to look at things from this perspective. The idea of "digging multiple wells" doesn't easily come to mind, and we normally aren't able to see past what seems to be the only choice in front of us.

For example, reaching an impasse in one's job or career is a common problem that can place us in a Hamlet-like predicament. We may struggle to get along with our superiors and subordinates, see no prospects for promotion, and lack enthusiasm for our work. We may want to leave our job, but doing so may jeopardize our livelihood and the welfare of our family.

In this dilemma, we have only two choices: either stay in our job and persevere until we can resolve our problems or break new ground elsewhere. But we can use lateral thinking to come up with different ways of deciding between the two possibilities. For example, we can choose to rely on our own judgment to make the decision, or we might choose to confide in a friend and ask for her input. We might also explore the possibility of a career change, in which case, we will need to examine which careers we are best suited for and determine our chances of succeeding in them. Finally, we may want to reconsider and thoroughly reexamine whether our current company might still hold possibilities for us after all.

As we explore the possibilities within each of these options, we will eventually find an open path. The key is not to be too single-minded. Instead, we must use lateral thinking to persistently search for new places to break ground. This, I believe, is also a secret to a successful life.

FOUR

The Keys to Succeeding in Business

Respecting Your Supervisor

There are many books on how to achieve success in business, but few, if any, mention respecting your supervisor as the first condition for success. But when we closely examine people who do not succeed at work, we find that they do not respect their superiors. In fact, respect for your supervisor is so crucial that I consider it the first key to success in business.

Of course, no one is perfect, so you will no doubt find faults and shortcomings in your supervisor. In fact, you probably have no trouble finding things about your supervisor to complain about. But there may be other, positive aspects of your supervisor that you are not seeing. The very fact that your supervisor has been placed above you means that someone in an even higher position recognizes his or her competency. If you feel that your supervisor is completely inept and you see nothing but his or her faults, chances are that you will not be able to get ahead in that organization.

Conversely, if you list your supervisor's strengths and weaknesses and find that the strengths far outnumber the weaknesses, you have a very good chance of being successful. Harboring an image of your supervisor as far less capable than you are will only give rise to a continuing sense of frustration, and your disrespectful attitude will most likely displease your supervisor, too. And when both parties are dissatisfied with each other, a working relationship cannot succeed.

If you feel that your supervisor does not deserve his or her current position, think about it this way: that position is the result of achievements and a performance that you have yet to achieve. Developing respect for your supervisor's competence is the first step to succeeding at work.

To better understand your relationship with your supervisor, imagine a master-apprentice situation. Even if certain things about the master bothered you, you would still listen to his or her advice. If you thought you had made a mistake, you would apologize. You should have the same kind of relationship with your supervisor at work. First, try regarding your supervisor as your master. Then adopt a humble attitude of learning from your supervisor what you have not yet learned.

You may well have the potential to become a great leader in your organization. Your supervisor, on the other hand, may be nearing retirement or even facing dismissal. But anyone can criticize; people of mediocre talent can still point out the faults of those who excel. In fact, many great figures in history have been condemned by ordinary people, and their criticism was not always unreasonable. This means that just as you can criticize your supervisor, your supervisor can criticize you, and that criticism may not be entirely off the mark. Your supervisor can easily spot your shortcomings, even if you are the more capable and competent one. When your supervisor reprimands you, admonishes you, or scolds you, instead of regarding it as unreasonable criticism, use it as an opportunity to ponder ways you might improve your work.

People who do not respect their supervisors are unlikely to become successful at work, because they are basically casting doubt on the decisions that the top executives have made. Someone in a higher position has promoted your supervisor to his or her current position, so disrespecting your supervisor ultimately means that you distrust a decision made by the top management.

If you disapprove of the person who is ultimately responsible for managing the organization, you're very unlikely to have a successful career in that company. But that doesn't mean that you or your company is to blame; it simply means that you and your company are not suited for each other. So the first key to success in business, whatever the industry or the organization you work for, is to learn to respect your superiors.

Cherishing Your Subordinates

Just as it is imperative to respect our superiors, cherishing our subordinates is crucial to our success. Some people mistakenly believe that it was their own ability alone that got them where they are now, but none of us can rise to greatness without the love and support of our subordinates. We may achieve temporary success, but we will eventually lose the trust of others and with it, our position of responsibility in our organization.

So how do we cherish our subordinates? We help them develop their strengths while guiding them to overcome their shortcomings. We may not always get to choose the people who work under us, but even so, it is our responsibility to help them grow so that they will become persons of noble character who will be capable of completing their work on their own. It is part of our job to help our subordinates develop their abilities and prepare them for promotion to higher positions.

When we guide others in this way, the most important thing to be careful about is to avoid becoming jealous of their talents. Some people feel threatened by highly capable subordinates and end up nitpicking everything they do in an effort to keep them from succeeding. This kind of behavior will probably succeed at preventing the subordinate from getting ahead in the company, but it will also hinder the supervisor's chances for promotion.

Those who achieve greatness treasure people for their aptitude. They value and appreciate others' unique and exceptional talents and gifts, whether or not they share those same talents and gifts. The truly great among us help others develop their potential.

To cherish your subordinates is to help them grow in their strengths while respecting their individuality and uniqueness. If one of our subordinates is much more talented and capable than we are, then we should be proud to have such an outstanding assistant. Only when we can develop such a state of mind can we achieve even greater success.

We cannot achieve success alone. We can only become successful with the support of others or a push from the people under us. We can only succeed by gaining others' trust. And our subordinates will not be willing to help us if we don't first cherish them. It is the support and approval of the people around us that leads to our own promotion to higher positions. Success comes when we become someone that others would like to work for.

The second key to success is so important that it's worth repeating again: we must cultivate the habit of discovering, praising and nurturing the exceptional talents and capabilities of those working under us. Appreciating the aptitudes of others, whether we share those same aptitudes or not, promotes our own development and spiritual growth.

Increasing the Value of Your Work

It can sometimes be frustrating if our colleagues earn a higher salary than we do, especially if we feel that we are putting more time and effort into the work than they are. Even if the difference in our take-home pay is as little as ten dollars a month, it may bother us. On the other hand, if we learn that our bonus was a hundred dollars more than what others received, we may feel gratified and tempted to boast about it. It may be human nature to feel restless about how high or low our pay is compared to others', but if we want to reach the height of excellence, we need to break away from this disposition and start thinking in a way that will truly benefit us.

If we feel that our hard work deserves higher pay, we should consider how much our company has already invested in us. Suppose we started working for our company as an entry-level employee and were paid and received bonuses even though we weren't yet bringing much profit to the company. If we include company benefits and other expenses, our company probably made a huge investment in us, because entry-level employees usually cannot earn their salaries' worth. So other, more experienced employees must have earned the profits necessary to compensate for the cost of our salary. This means that when we gain knowledge, skills, and experiences after several years of working at our company, we need to start generating enough profit to pay not only our own salary, but also the salaries of employees who are not yet competent enough to earn their keep.

If we want to become successful, we should strive to work five or ten times more than we do now so that we can clearly distinguish ourselves from others. As a rough guideline, we should aim to produce profits or results that are worth ten times the amount we earn.

No company wants to let go of employees who bring in profits that are worth ten times their salaries. If you see no prospect of getting ahead in your company after doing this for one, two, or three years, then you're probably not in the right company for you, and you can probably find a better job that will allow you to make better use of your potential.

But most people feel frustrated by subtle differences between the effort they put in to their work and the compensation they receive. They may complain that, for example, they have worked 20 percent harder than others but have received only 10 percent more in their bonus. But complaining about such a trivial issue is exactly why they don't see an increase in their pay. If you are unhappy because you feel that the little extra effort you've made is not being recognized, it may simply mean that you're not aware of how companies function.

When we work for a company or organization, it is simply not good enough to work just to earn our salary's worth. We need to produce profits at least several times greater than what we receive so that we can support people working in sections that do not directly generate profits but are necessary for the company to continue functioning. To put it another way, you should try to become someone that your company feels grateful to have. Never become a burden; instead become a benefactor to the company. Become a powerful and positive driving force that can lead others and improve everyone's lives.

True success comes to those who bring positive changes to the lives of the people around them. So instead of focusing only on how you can improve the quality of your life, think about how you can benefit your company so that the profits you make will pay for the wages of everyone in your office.

This kind of positive and constructive thinking will help improve the lives of not only your colleagues, but also, eventually, the rest of the world. Unhappiness and darkness will not disappear as long as we're only concentrating on lighting up our own small space. The world will become a brighter, happier place when each one of us increases our light by tenfold to brighten the lives of those around us.

To enhance your prospects for success, make it your principle to produce ten times more than what you receive. When I say this, however, I am not referring to the time you spend at work; I am not suggesting that you work ten times longer than you do now. After all, there are only twenty-four hours in a day; no one can shorten or extend the time we are given. Even if we want to work more hours, we can really only extend our workday by several hours at most. Instead, we need to increase the value of our work by maximizing our efficiency and productivity, which we do by focusing on completing our most important tasks. We should also keep striving to improve by trying out new approaches and creative ideas.

Making the Most of
Your Unique Strengths

Once we have put into practice the first three keys to success in business—respecting our superiors, cherishing our subordinates, and increasing the value of our work—the most crucial thing to focus on is using our strengths—the unique gifts that we are born with.

We each have a unique character, and that is a good thing. But conflicts often occur when individuals try to express their uniqueness. Self-willed people in particular cause friction with others, because they tend to force their opinions and resist yielding to other people's wishes. Conformity becomes an essential element in avoiding conflicts, and people who work to avoid standing out usually do well in large corporations.

Getting ahead in a large corporation often requires social skills that involve ingratiating ourselves with our superiors while at the same time becoming popular among our subordinates. As a result, those working for large organizations often develop a tendency to suppress their individuality, and some may feel frustrated that they are not able to express themselves in their work.

But if we want to live a fulfilling life that makes us feel happy that we lived, it is essential that we make the most of our unique talents. So how do we make the best use of our gifts and strengths in a corporate setting? By delivering concrete results that withstand criticism. If you are truly contributing to the growth of your company, it becomes extremely difficult for naysayers to keep ignoring, criticizing, or devaluing your efforts. But if you try to bring forward your abilities without producing concrete results that clearly benefit your company, it will be easy for others to misunderstand you, and you may find yourself confronted with difficult situations.

Recognizable achievements should be the basis of expressing your unique character. So if you want to make the most of your unique abilities and express your personality at work, strive to produce strong results so that no one can deny your efforts. Work steadily to establish a record of achievements that everyone can objectively recognize as great contributions to the company.

And when the time comes for you to exert your unique abilities, it is important to do so in a quiet fashion. Express your ability slowly and carefully, as if you are lighting a candle inside you. Gradually increase the size of the candle's flame until it becomes bright enough to light up the world outside you.

If you flare up your flame of enthusiasm all at once in the beginning of your career, your coworkers may see you as a nuisance. So start off with a small spark, and let out your talent little by little as you accumulate concrete results. Eventually, it will become obvious to everyone that you have amassed a record of achievements. Soon, you will be able to carry out your work in your own way without others noticing.

Some people, when they are elevated to a higher position, try to do everything their way from the start. But when opportunity knocks, it's best to act with prudence. Observe how your predecessor handled similar projects, listen to the opinions of others, and carry out your new responsibilities quietly, humbly, and discreetly. Then, as you find your feet, you will soon be able to work intensively to make full use of your talent.

Constantly Improving

The fifth key to success in business is working to improve every day. This may sound easy to do, especially when we first take on a new job. But after a while, it's easy to get stuck in routine work. The risk of this is that after a few years of doing the same tasks over and over, we may find ourselves losing interest in our work.

But to be exceptional, we need to make an effort to keep thinking of new ideas and new ways to improve our work and maintain an unfading enthusiasm—even when people around us lose motivation, fall into laziness, and start putting more energy on leisure activities.

As a matter of course, constantly striving to improve helps us do our work more efficiently and productively. But beyond these benefits, an enthusiastic attitude of constant improvement can act as a powerful stimulant that positively influences those around us, motivating them to keep improving as well. It's not only the bad stuff that spreads; good things are contagious, too.

We can be creative and innovative in many different situations, even while working on the simplest tasks, but no one really teaches us how to do that. The best way to bring innovation to our work is by either thinking through how to solve a specific problem or considering whether we could handle a situation we're facing in a new and unique way.

For example, a worker may feel frustrated with how ineffi-cient he is and may not know why. But people around him may be able to spot the problem and find a solution right away. It may be something as simple as sorting documents into a "to-do" tray and a "done" tray. He may be having difficulty prioritizing his work and so ends up wasting time. Or maybe he spends too much time on the phone, and by changing how he handles phone calls—for example, getting right to the topic and keeping the conversation as concise as possible—he can shorten the time he spends on phone calls and make more time for other tasks.

We can come up with new ideas not only by building up our knowledge base on subjects connected to our work, but also by learning from others how they handle their work. Based on my observations of the people I've worked with in the business world, I have learned that people who devote themselves solely to their own work do not achieve outstanding accomplishments. On the other hand, those who pay attention to what others are doing and learn from them often achieve excellence.

We can gain ingenious ideas for our work by interacting with our coworkers and paying close attention to how they work, how they talk, and any new information that they share. Making small, everyday changes, such as adopting someone else's eloquent way of speaking on the phone, can gradually turn us into extraordinary people. If we constantly learn from others about how they make decisions and develop new ideas and incorporate these ideas into our own work, we will become more capable and will eventually develop our original style and approach to work.

We are not supposed to use our eyes only to look at what's in front of us; we're supposed to use them to observe what others are doing. The same is true for our ears. We should use our ears to listen to what others are saying. Making these kinds of small but constant efforts to improve is crucial to our success.

In addition, we should always be thinking about what is on the minds of people in higher positions and what we can do to help them. Putting ourselves in our bosses' shoes and constantly considering what sort of help they need from us helps us unleash our creativity and develop new and innovative ideas.

Elevating Your Outlook on Life

I sincerely wish for all my readers to become successful at work, but that doesn't mean that I'm suggesting either that they simply be competent at what they do or that they become workaholics. We cannot measure our success only by our level of usefulness. No matter how capable we are, success can be far from our reach if we are disliked as a person or if others feel uncomfortable being around us and feel a sense of relief when we leave the office.

Work is a place where we can accumulate life experience, and so it is also a place where we can share spiritual Truths with others. We human beings are always influencing one another through our daily conversations and interactions. The words we speak have the power to lead others. That's why it is crucial that we study people to learn from their life philosophies, instead of just trying to learn skills and knowledge specific to our job. And while it's wonderful to learn from people who are more capable than we are, we can also learn from those who are not as competent as we are. We can learn from their strengths and even from their mistakes by examining why they made such mistakes.

Our work environment gives us an opportunity to meet and work with an incredibly diverse range of people that we can learn from. Knowing different types of people and their unique characters can help us in many ways. We should particularly focus on learning the basic thinking and behavioral patterns of different people. By deepening our understanding of different ways of thinking, we can accumulate knowledge and turn it into experiences. There is no limit to the depth of knowledge we can acquire. As we deepen the level of our understanding, we will be able to improve ourselves as human beings.

We should not be content just to do our job right. I believe it is just as, if not more, important to grow spiritually and develop a broader perspective on life through our daily work.

Devoting Yourself to the Divine

The seventh key to success is good advice for those who have already been practicing the first six keys. If you are one of these people, you have probably achieved a certain level of success at work and have begun to stand out from your colleagues. But it is when we become confident of our capability that we are on the verge of falling into a pitfall. Feeling as if we know exactly what others are thinking and that everything we do is sure to succeed is a sign of conceit. We may feel this way simply because we have a limited view of the world; we only know what we've done so far and aren't aware of all the other areas in which we lack experience.

If you feel that you have achieved victory in the small world of your business, step outside and visit the rest of the world. The world is much bigger than you think. Look up at the night sky from time to time and feel the vastness of the universe. Ponder the mystery of the universe and contemplate its laws. Ask yourself for what purpose we human beings are born into this world and why we die. What is the meaning of our life in this world if it is going to eventually end? What is the significance of all the works and achievements that the generations before us created? Look at this world from a higher perspective and consider, from time to time, all the people you work with, including even some of the people you don't get along with, as fellow crewmembers on this spaceship called Earth.

What I am trying to say here is that we should never forget to revere the Divine. As we move up into management positions and become responsible for a larger number of people, we need to increasingly deepen our devotion to the Divine, the existence that transcends human understanding. We may sometimes feel as if human beings are almighty, but when we believe in the existence of the Higher Being or God and become aware of the broader perspective of this great existence, we will realize how small our own existence really is.

In other words, we should never forget to be humble. The higher we climb on the ladder of success, the more humble we should become. We should become more selfless and unpretentious as we progress toward higher awareness. This humility will help us pursue ever-higher goals, overcome our weaknesses and shortcomings, and keep improving ourselves.

True success in business is possible only when we become aware that life is something that we have been given and that we only continue to live because of the help we receive from all creation and the will of the Great Universe.

Achieving success that can only be measured in numbers does not guarantee success in the truest sense. No matter how brilliant your accomplishments may appear to be, you will one day leave the business world. What will stay with you when you go? What can you leave behind as proof of your existence? What are the things that no one else but you could bring into the world? This is the perspective that we should always keep in mind as we climb up the ladder of success. We can achieve true success when we bring about good results with a humble attitude and a devotion to manifesting and realizing Divine Will.

Leaving Behind a Spiritual Legacy

The last key to success that I would like to discuss is considering what kind of spiritual legacy we can leave behind through our work, regardless of our occupation, position, or title. Through the course of our life in this world, we leave behind a record of our spiritual journey. And there will be a time when we have to review our life and ponder what gifts we were able to share with those we met along the way.

When we do this, we will inevitably find ourselves noticing the many mistakes we have made throughout our life. We may feel ashamed of our own silliness and feel as though we can never escape from our own failures. But when we feel helpless about the mistakes we've made, we should try to make up for them, and the way we do that is leaving behind something that benefits others.

The best gift we can pass on to others is a spiritual one. A spiritual gift will leave a heavenly scent in the hearts of those who come in contact with us during the course of our life, including our supervisor, our assistants, and our colleagues. No matter what role someone has in our life, we should always aim to leave behind a gift in their heart so that they feel glad to have met or worked with us. A life lived without leaving behind such a spiritual gift is futile. We should live with a wish to share such a heavenly gift with each and every person we meet, at every opportunity we're given. This gift will touch their heart and refresh their mind like a May breeze and will stay with them, however faintly, long after we are gone.

There may be a limit to what we can do for those we meet through our work, but we can at least cast a compassionate eye on everyone. We can listen to everyone we meet, feel their sorrows, and understand their sufferings, and we can offer them words of encouragement and support. I sincerely hope that many people will be able to leave behind these spiritual gifts, because this is the surest way to great success.

FIVE

The Gate to Economic Prosperity

What Is Economic Activity?

To begin this chapter, let us ponder the role that economic activities play in our society. The money-based economy was developed relatively recently in the timeline of human history. But even before we started using money as a medium of exchange, human beings had economic systems. Economic activities—assessing the value of our daily labor, saving what we earn, and exchanging it for something of equal value—give rise to an economic system.

I am not an adherent of the old-fashioned labor theory of value, but I believe that at the basis of economic activities lie human activities that have value that we can assess objectively. In other words, actions that are valuable to us personally but that lack objective value are not economic activities.

Fishing, for instance, can be considered an economic activity because the fish caught have objective value. The fisher can either sell the fish or trade them for something of equal value. Even if he decides to eat the fish himself, they still have economic value, because he no longer has to purchase or obtain the other food that he would need if he didn't eat the fish. In this respect, the fish has an equal value to what the fisher would have spent for his meal.

What kinds of human activities do not have objective value? Let's say that a person spends all his time studying worms. In itself, this is not an economic activity. But if, as a consequence of this study, he discovers how to breed worms in large quantity, he can turn his hobby into an economic activity. For instance, he might sell the worms to a practitioner of traditional Chinese medicine or make use of the nutrient-filled soil that the worms inhabit. In this way, we can transform actions that originally have no objective value into economic activities.

Economic activities don't have to involve currency, but they have to provide some kind of good or service that has an objective value to others. Inuits, for example, didn't use money; instead, their economic system was based on bartering: they traded seal meat, pelt, and fur for other necessities. This kind of exchange of goods is economic activity because the sealskin and meat are valuable to them and to others.

In short, an economic activity is a human activity that produces objective value that both we and others can appreciate.

What Is Value?

What, then, makes something valuable? I believe that there are two essential elements of value. The first is *usefulness*—the intrinsic value of the good or service. Take fruits for example. Fruits are edible and provide fiber and vitamins that are good for our health. Likewise, cows, milk, chicken, and eggs are all intrinsically valuable.

The second element is *acknowledgment*, or our recognition of the value of the good or service. Diamonds are a good example of this. From the standpoint of usefulness, a pair of scissors or a sewing kit is more valuable than a diamond is. But we all know that diamonds are much more valuable. This is because we *find* great value in diamonds.

We place a high value on diamonds for two reasons: their beauty and their rarity. If diamonds were everywhere, like pebbles on riverbeds, we probably wouldn't place such a high value on them; instead, we'd probably get tired of looking at them and treat them as insignificant, like rubbish. If we were constantly surrounded by diamonds, we might even complain that their brilliant shine hurts our eyes. But we find diamonds valuable because they are both rare and beautiful. Diamonds may not have intrinsic value, as eggs and milk do, but they are worth a lot because we acknowledge and appreciate them as valuable.

From another perspective, however, both the egg and the diamond have value by and of themselves; the only difference may be whether that value is something that everyone acknowledges or something that only some people recognize.

Another type of value is produced through human actions. Manufacturing techniques can transform raw materials into useful objects. For example, we can create a useful tool from a lump of plain iron. We can increase the value of thread by weaving it into cloth. In this way, we can transform a material of low value into an object of higher value. The object becomes more valuable not because we develop a liking for it but because human activity transforms it into something that serves a purpose. In any case, we create value when our work creates demand—that is, when it makes a lot of people eager to obtain what we have produced.

Truth Value and Utopia Value

The phrase *added value* is often used in economics to refer to what our work adds to the value of a product or service. Added value plays a significant role in today's economy. For example, a plain white shirt may sell for ten dollars, but when we add elaborate embroidery to it, the price may double or triple. We can further raise the price by giving it a unique design.

A while back, a Japanese economist predicted the coming of the "knowledge-value-based era," in which consumers would pay for the value of knowledge and ideas. He cited designer brands as an example of such value. If we consider ties, for example, there should not be much difference in the cost of the material that ties are made of, but ties by designers such as Gucci and Hermes have much higher prices than non-designer ties. This is how intangible ideas add value to a product.

But I don't think that this "knowledge value" alone would ever be sufficient to become the sole basis of our economic activities. I say this because I believe that what matters now is the *nature* of the knowledge we can bring to our activities. What we need now is not simple knowledge, but wisdom that will contribute to the development and evolution of the laws that govern this great universe. We should assess the value of our economic activities based on *Truth value*, as I call it, instead of knowledge value.

In some cases, ideas, goods, and services that people produce by working to improve things may actually harm others. For instance, let's say that a particular factory believes that its new cost-cutting methods are valuable to the company. But the way they cut costs is by neglecting proper treatment of the wastewater, and instead discharging it to the local rivers, causing harm to the people living in the vicinity. In this case, their idea is not valuable from the perspective of Truth value, because it ends up harming people. So it is not the knowledge or idea per se, but its nature that determines whether it truly creates value.

Today, Western individualism pervades the world. Individualism advocates that individuals take the initiative to engage in activities that bring them profits, higher status, and respect for their achievements. But as long as our actions are based on selfish motives, our outlook will remain bleak. We should use our knowledge, ideas, and wisdom to benefit the whole of society and to contribute to the development of the entire human race. Only then will our knowledge create added value for all.

To expand on this idea, I would like to introduce the term *utopia value*. This concept helps us see economic activities from the viewpoint of how much we contribute to the creation of an ideal world. To use the example of ties again, a designer tie may make us look sophisticated and attractive. But it may not have a high utopia value—that is, it may not contribute much to the world.

Another example might be books. The price of a book is generally determined based on the cost of printing, paper, and promotion. However, two books with the same price may not have the same utopia value. One book might contribute greatly to the happiness of humankind, while the other one may be harmful to our well-being. In terms of their relative utopia value, one could be worth ten times more than the other, even if they have the same price tag at the store.

I believe that our economic activities should be based on a new study of economics that pursues *Truth value* and *utopia value*. I predict the coming of an era in which religious leaders work with economists to bring forth such a value system.

What Is Economic Prosperity?

How would you define economic prosperity? I believe that we can achieve economic prosperity at multiple levels. At the individual level, each of us can achieve prosperity in our personal finances. At the corporate level, our companies and organizations can thrive and become prosperous. At the country level, our local regions and nations can become prosperous. At the multinational, continental level, international entities such as the European Union can prosper. And finally, at the global level, we can achieve economic prosperity on a planetary scale.

Economic prosperity has two essential characteristics. First, from a purely scientific view, we have economic prosperity when we have more and more people and goods moving within a certain time and space. Economic prosperity occurs when there is a drastic boost in the flow of people and goods in a country, region, or organization during a fixed period of time. These intense activities lead to an increased flow of money, the medium of exchange we use to pay for goods, services, and labor. So economic prosperity entails abundant exchanges, transfers, and other activities involving *people, goods, money*, and, in today's society, *information*. In times of economic prosperity, we see these four elements moving and circulating rapidly.

We can also define economic prosperity subjectively, from the perspective of the people who are experiencing it. In prosperous times, the people who are active in generating the economy find great satisfaction in their work and hold great hope for the future. People find purpose in their work, believe that their prospects are bright, and have high expectations for good job opportunities, business development, and economic expansion.

Finally, we can define economic prosperity from a spiritual perspective. Human beings are essentially spiritual beings that incarnate into this world, live a temporary life, and return to the spirit world after death. We are prosperous when our souls are rejoicing and shining brilliantly. We are living in times of economic prosperity when we are imprinting on our souls the value and joy of living a life full of profound and precious experiences of energy and vigor.

Prosperity Attracts Further Prosperity

Economic prosperity is subject to the law of attraction: prosperity attracts further prosperity. When a business starts to go well, all the element of economic prosperity improve for that business—people, goods, money, and information. And the people involved in the business find motivation, fulfillment, and enthusiasm in their work.

When a worker's eyes sparkle with joy as she does her job, her positive energy gradually spreads to her coworkers, and the whole workplace becomes vibrant with vitality. This positive atmosphere draws more and more people to want to be part of it, leading the organization to greater success. This is an example of how prosperity attracts further prosperity.

This same law of attraction works for wealth, as well: wealth attracts more wealth. There are three types of wealth. The first is financial wealth. The second is wealth of knowledge, which can also be referred to as wisdom or sometimes as wits. This sort of knowledge can be useful in various situations in life. The third type is the wealth of human resources. When a large number of people engage in an organization's work, that organization has a wealth of human resources.

Prosperity attracts further prosperity when these three elements—financial wealth, wealth of knowledge, and wealth of human resources—create positive synergy. To achieve economic prosperity, we need to use one of these elements, or a combination of two or three of them, to move in a better direction as a whole. For instance, with financial wealth, we can consolidate our prosperity by employing outstanding personnel or using the funds to gain information, knowledge, and know-how in a variety of fields.

Even if we don't have financial capital, we can still use the other two elements to achieve economic prosperity. If we have a stock of knowledge or ideas, we can start a new business. Many of today's most successful businesses started with a simple idea or a thought in someone's mind. Good ideas attract collaborators and funds. If we have a wealth of knowledge, we can use it as capital to create substantial prosperity.

Securing excellent human capital can also bring about economic prosperity. With the help of brilliant people, we can start any kind of business. Even if we lack both funds and expertise, we can still start a new project, as long as we have a group of talented people to help us with it. In fact, outstanding personnel are often necessary to the success of a start-up business. In starting a new business, you may be a novice in the field, and you may have limited funds to draw on, but your chance of success is high if you have excellent personnel.

In today's rapidly changing society, people are prone to change jobs. Some succeed at their new job, while others fail. But those who succeed are often those who succeeded in their previous jobs as well. Such people have the confidence that comes from having experienced success in the past. The people around them also recognize their ability to do well in a particular field.

New businesses can succeed by hiring capable, competent, talented people, even if all their previous success has been in a completely different field. For instance, a preparatory school in Japan expanded its business rapidly after recruiting a hotshot from a stock company. Bringing in a distinguished individual from a different field can bring about a drastic transformation in the company, producing completely unexpected results.

I would like to emphasize again the importance of these three elements—funds, knowledge or ideas, and human resources—as essential for achieving prosperity. Having all three ensures success, but even with only one of them, we can open a path to prosperity.

The Four Conditions of True Prosperity

I would like to conclude this chapter with a discussion of true prosperity. As I said earlier, prosperity is a state which people, goods, money, and information circulate at high speed within a set period of time and space and the people involved are filled with hope and enthusiasm. I would now like to consider economic prosperity from a different perspective: the perspective of human growth.

I believe that to achieve prosperity and become successful in the truest sense, we need to meet four conditions. First, others must recognize our success. It is not enough to claim that we have succeeded; our work must be objectively successful in the eyes of society. We should trust society's assessment of our accomplishments. True prosperity should accompany the acknowledgement of our success by the majority of people in society.

Societal recognition is an important tool for gauging our success, and this is true not only in terms of the recognition that we receive for our worldly achievements, but also for success that has spiritual value. For instance, if someone achieves financial prosperity through criminal behavior, society should not recognize it as true success. Similarly, huge profits from wildcat real estate speculation should not be considered true prosperity. Financial success from illicit gain at the expense of others should only result in a bad reputation. So while societal recognition is not the sole factor that determines our success, it is still important that sensible people recognize our achievements.

The second condition of true prosperity is the growth and development of our character. Lasting prosperity requires constant personal improvement. As a company grows, so should the person in charge. A company will grow consistently as long as its director continues to think in a way that suits the scale of the business and continues to innovate and improve.

The third condition of true prosperity is social influence that corresponds to our level of wealth. Having a large nest egg in our bank account isn't enough to make us truly prosperous. We need to exert a positive impact on society by making use of our accumulated wealth, social prestige, fame, and other factors to benefit society.

The fourth condition of true prosperity is a life of no regrets. No matter how much profit we're bringing in, we are not achieving true prosperity unless we find purpose and meaning in our work. Even an unprecedented business opportunity that guarantees overwhelming financial success will not make us spiritually prosperous if the goal we are seeking to achieve does not accord with the natural inclination of our soul.

For example, if someone who is devoutly pursuing spiritual values enters into a business venture and spends all his time seeking profits, he will feel empty inside and regret wasting his life. Each soul has unique characteristics of its own, and souls with an affinity for religion, spirituality, or philosophy are usually not suited to speculative business. The success we achieve in an area that does not align with our natural inclinations will become a source of pain in the long run.

Finding success in a field that suits the characteristics of our souls is essential to living a life with no regrets. So to fulfill the fourth condition of true prosperity, we need to find jobs that will actively lead to the evolution of our soul. If you don't feel that your current job will help you grown spiritually, you will eventually need to shift your career direction. In that case, I suggest that you begin by building a foundation of financial success and then look for the next step to take.

SIX

The Power of Developmental Thinking

The Miraculous Power of Thoughts

This chapter examines one of the functions of the human mind: *thinking*. This exploration will play an important role in understanding the principles of success in today's world.

I would like to start by talking about how our thoughts work. *Thoughts* can also be referred to as *concepts plus will*. While concepts are broad ideas, will is more focused and has a clear objective. So thoughts are broad ideas that are fixed in a set direction. In this context, the word *thoughts* means basically the same thing as *life plan*, which is our vision for the future developed into specific ideas about how we want to live. This vision becomes powerful when we embrace it constantly and persistently every day.

Most people today are not aware of the power of thoughts. But our thoughts have immense potential and can even take on a physical force. Our thoughts work in a similar way as the blueprint of a house. We need a plan or blueprint to construct a house. Similarly, the thoughts we hold in our mind construct our life.

A blueprint takes on a life of its own when our will drives us to carry out the actions necessary to build the house, such as getting an estimate for the construction cost, acquiring the necessary funds, and hiring people to build it. Just as our children grow up and start living on their own, our thoughts start working on their own the moment we conceive them. This is creation; this is how we produce things from scratch.

Thoughts are invisible and inaudible, so most of us have never heard or seen them. But with spiritual eyes, we can see that images and ideas projected from our minds float in the air and travel around the world. We are surrounded by whorls of people's thoughts, and our thoughts influence one another as they give rise to new creation.

Let me use the metaphor of a house and its blueprint to explain how this works. Suppose an ambitious young woman draws a blueprint of a house and displays it where others can see it. A passerby notices it and thinks, "That would be a very nice house. I would love to see it built." The passerby then visits the woman and finds out that this talented young architect doesn't have the funds to build the house. Upon hearing this, the man says, "I can see that you have a bright future ahead of you as an architect, so I would like to help you build this house and make your dream come true."

He then brings his friends to see the blueprint and asks them to help him build the house. One of his friends says, "Let me take care of the funds. I can finance half of it myself, and with my credit, I can borrow the rest from the bank." Another friend says, "I know a good carpenter. He should be able to start working on it sometime this month. I'll get in touch with him right away."

We need a blueprint because simply saying that we want to construct a building does not get us the specific help we need. A clear vision of our intentions attracts people who are interested in our dreams and able to support them. If we keep explaining to people how our building will look, where we plan to build it, and what its purpose will be, those who are not interested will simply pass by, but those who are interested will find it fascinating. If our building is a factory for Persian carpets, an interior designer might be attracted to it and even offer help. She might also share your idea with her friends, and they might offer to pitch in too.

Setting clearly defined goals is a powerful act: it sets your focus and captivates the imaginations of like-minded others, both of which increase the chances that your dream will take shape. If you hold onto a concrete vision of what you wish to achieve and share your vision with others, those who are inspired by your vision will help you make it a reality.

Your clear vision will attract not only people in this world, but also beings in the invisible world that exist beyond this material world. Although most people are not aware of their existence, we all have a guardian spirit and guiding spirits who watch over us and try to help us from the spirit world. Holding a clear and strong vision helps us receive the aid of these beings in the fourth and higher dimensions. The first step to making our dreams come true is recognizing the power of our thoughts.

Manifesting Our Thoughts

We often hold vague images of what we want to create, but it is difficult and often takes advanced skills and training to actually create those things in real life. The practical challenges of realizing our vision can lead us into negative thinking. If we wish to build a house, for example, within a day or two, we may start thinking, "There is no way I can afford to build a house with my income, and I have no one to help me financially." This negation destroys the vision in our mind.

The most essential key for manifesting our thoughts is to keep envisioning them as time passes. Don't set a specific time limit for achieving your goal. There is no need to corner yourself that way. Just hold on to the idea in your mind and hope that it will be realized when the time comes. As long as you keep envisioning your dream, things will begin to move in the right direction to make it come true. You may come into contact with people who will help you achieve your dream, or you may be given opportunities that will lead you to a path of success.

Imprint in your heart this point: your thoughts require an extended period of time to manifest. If you hold on to a specific idea for at least three years, chances are that it will come true some way or other, even if it doesn't happen exactly as you envisioned it. If you hold onto your vision for ten years, it is extremely unlikely that it will not come true. That is because a lot of people today, especially in advanced countries, are looking for opportunities to cooperate with others to achieve success.

Nothing is impossible when we can get all the help we need from those who are willing to help make our dreams come true. Even if you see yourself as an ordinary person with no special talent, you will be able to start a business, succeed in it, and leave something for posterity if you can just keep a mental vision of your dream for ten years.

Conversely, if you let go of your vision half way through, you might move further away from your goal. An abandoned hope is like a bulletin board after a notice has been removed. Your potential collaborator may pass by the bulletin board but now has no way of knowing what the notice said. A notice that says "Room Wanted" or "Situation Wanted" will catch people's attention as long as it is posted on the bulletin board. If you take it off, even if someone who can provide exactly what you need is standing in front of the bulletin board, she will never see the notice and so will not be able to give you anything. As this analogy illustrates, persistently and continually holding a vision of your dream is essential to making it come true.

The Power of Positive Images

Now that I've discussed the power of our thoughts and explained how the images we hold in our mind can become real, there is another essential point I would like you to remember: only positive thoughts can bring happiness to ourselves and others. Put another way, negative thoughts can have a self-destructive power.

Based on my observations, many people, perhaps more than half or even two-thirds of the population, hold onto unhappy images of themselves. What these people have in common is that they all carry scars from their past. They have experienced failures or setbacks that make them feel as though they are bound to fail no matter how many times they try to lead a successful life. Even if they are in a completely new situation and dealing with new people, they can't escape the feeling that they're going to make the same exact mistakes they made in the past.

Someone who has experienced the trauma of being fired will be nervous about losing his job no matter where he works. This fear will eventually manifest itself. He will fall in a vicious cycle of being repeatedly fired as long as he holds onto this fear. Similarly, those who are forever worrying about falling ill invite sickness. Those who carry a pessimistic outlook invite failure. Those who are paranoid that they are being betrayed will sooner or later be let down.

This principle can also work in the opposite direction to create a cycle of goodness. Those who have been successful in one job will continue to be successful when they change jobs. The difference between these two types of people is the image they have in mind: positive or negative.

Essentially, however, the root of negative thoughts may not be solely your past experiences of failure. A negative self-image actually stems from a lack of self-confidence. This diffidence might not even be attributable to mental causes; it could be something physical—for example, you may simply be feeling a bit under the weather. We often dwell in negative thoughts when we are exhausted, worn-out, depressed, or totally unmotivated. Conversely, it's hard to feel negative and pessimistic when we are in good shape and wake up in the morning filled with energy and ready to start a hard day's work.

Physical well-being is essential to feeling positive about ourselves. If you feel that you have a tendency to be pessimistic, I suggest that you build up your physical strength and lead a healthy life. If you neglect your physical health and focus only on your mental state, you may gradually develop negative thoughts without realizing it.

In addition to building up your physical strength, another way of maintaining a positive vision in your mind is to keep making discoveries and coming up with creative and new ideas every day. Setting new goals and making new discoveries on a daily basis will let us create a positive aura. We will remain unaffected by the pessimism of others as long as we never let any failures discourage us and instead keep trying out new ideas, one after another. This attitude is essential to achieving success.

We should avoid harboring negative thoughts, because negative thoughts attract failure. The human mind works like a magnet that attracts like-minded people. Those who carry around mental images of failure draw in the very people who are likely to cause the disaster they most fear. In contrast, pessimists hesitate to approach those who hold mental images of success because of the gap in their values and auras. This is how positive people sometimes manage to escape ill fortune.

Whether we succeed or fail in business largely depends on the kind of people we work with. In many cases, misjudgment in business relationships invites catastrophic failures. Constantly holding a positive, affirmative, and clear vision of our goal is critical to our success, because these images attract capable, positive, and proactive people who can help bring our hopes into reality.

To embrace positive and cheerful thoughts, it is essential to build up a number of successful experiences, however small those successes are. Try to achieve small successes by holding a positive image in your mind. For instance, let's say you have to give a sales pitch, but you have no confidence in your ability to pull it off. All you have to do to use the power of your mind is imagine yourself in a positive light, having successfully finished your presentation and landed a big account, and returning to the office with the great news. If you approach the deal confidently, with a firm conviction that you have already won it, your client will be so impressed and fascinated by your confident and relaxed demeanor that they will want to not only do business with you, but also get to know you outside of business.

The secret to success in business is impressing your clients or customers. You have already taken the first step toward success if you can get them to take interest in you as a person, or if you can make them want to learn more about you and build a long-lasting relationship with you. By constantly holding a positive vision, you will bring out the magnetic charm of your character and attract success.

Developmental Thinking

Once we have successfully created a positive vision in our mind, we can proceed to the next step: developmental thinking. Creating positive images in our mind is like knowing the best tactics for solving our day-to-day problems, and it can be extremely useful in our personal journey toward success. Developmental thinking, on the other hand, is more like a strategic plan that can be used by corporations, societies, and nations. With developmental thinking, we use the power of a positive vision that's held not just by an individual, but by a number of people working together.

Imagine that hundreds or even thousands of people are all sharing the same vision. If they maintain that vision for a period of time, it will become an immense power that can serve as a huge source of energy and creative force. In the world of religion, this is known as the power of faith. And even the business world can use this power of faith when the entire workforce of a corporation or organization shares the same positive image of success.

There is a simple way to assess a company's potential for success: look into the faces of every employee, and see whether they are brimming with hope and positive energy and whether there is a positive atmosphere in the office. When all the employees are happy and full of hope, the company will surely succeed. Even if a few people fall down on the job, the smiles of the rest of the staff will cancel them out.

In this sense, *developmental thinking* is a synonym for *management thinking*. It involves thinking about how to bring together every member of the organization to share a bright vision, or positive images, of the development of the business as a whole. Developmental thinking helps managers boost company morale because such thinking motivates and energizes everyone to aspire to higher goals.

There are three essential keys to developmental thinking. The first is to come up with a plan or vision on a grand scale. The leader's vision must be lofty and worthy of becoming the ideal of everyone in the organization. The second key is to set a deadline for the fruition of the goal. Most people find it difficult to envision a dream that will take ten or twenty years to realize. But if the leader can set a goal that the company can achieve within one to three years, the employees can focus on that goal. It is essential that the leader set a goal whose outcome will be recognizable to the workers so that they will be motivated to make the necessary effort to achieve it.

The third key is to make sure that, once the goal has been achieved, everyone who helped envision it gets to savor the joy of its fruition in some way. The leader needs to let the people reap the benefits of their contribution to the company's success. For example, workers could be promoted, be given a raise, or simply enjoy being part of a company whose status in society has risen. In one way or another, the leader should give back to the people who helped the leader achieve the goal by visualizing its success.

Managing the power of thoughts at an organizational level is essential to the organization's development. Anyone can picture success, but it is difficult to constantly and continually hold onto that picture. The leader needs to guide the workers to maintain the vision of success, amass their thoughts, and transform those thoughts into a great force that will bring about success. As long as the leader is full of enthusiasm and wins all the employees' support for the company goal, the company will no doubt greatly increase its sales. This is why those in leadership positions should practice developmental thinking.

The Alchemy of Looking at
the Bright Side

Let us now approach developmental thinking from another angle. Developmental thinking is a straightforward and direct approach to achieving our goals. But the path to success can often be bumpy and winding, so we need to think of measures to regain our footing in case we stumble along the way. No matter how passionate we are, we are bound to face various problems and setbacks, whether business or personal, so we need to prepare ourselves by learning how to rise above adversities.

What can help us when we face difficulties and hardships is looking at the bright side of things; it is shifting our perspective so that we can see things in a positive light.

Let us apply this attitude to a practical situation. Suppose you are in charge of the accounting department and your assistant makes a big mistake, causing the company to run a huge deficit. As his supervisor, you can deal with the situation in several ways. The first approach is to simply recognize it as a failure and wait until you can regain lost ground. Another approach is to fire the person responsible for the mistake or relegate him to a lower position. These are probably the simplest and most natural courses of action that would spring to anyone's mind if something like this were to happen.

But when you look at the situation in a positive light, you will see a completely different course of action. You will be able to think about how to use this devastating mistake as an opportunity for further growth.

It may be easier to simply fire the worker or demote him to a different division, but that would risk plunging him into despair. However, you cannot just let go and act as if nothing happened after such a terrible mistake. So it is up to you, as his supervisor, to decide how he should be treated.

First, ask yourself what you can do to help the person who made the mistake more successfully contribute to the company in the future. To decide what would be best for him, you need to examine his personality carefully and closely. If he is very proud, you should be careful not to make him lose face in front of everyone. If you reprimand him in public, he will get discouraged and may eventually leave the company. Instead, you should let him know that you have high expectations for him and encourage him to do better. For example, you could say something like, "It's not like you to make this kind of mistake. I have great hopes for you, and I trust that you will do your best to make up for this. I'm sure that you will be able to bring a lot of success to the company. I'm counting on you."

If he is not so proud and lacks the education and training he would need to improve his work skills, explain to him step by step where he went wrong and what he should have done. By showing him where he failed in his responsibilities, you can train him not to repeat the same mistake. To this type of person, you can perhaps say, "I will tolerate this mistake twice, but not a third time. Bear this in mind." In any case, it is essential to observe the worker as an individual and find the most effective way to bring out his best.

This same principle can also be applied on a larger, organizational level. If you fail in business, consider why it happened, and use it as a lesson to keep it from happening again. Check to see whether you might be making the same kind of mistake in a different area and whether the people you work with might make the same mistake. By doing this, you will be able to systematically improve the accuracy and the quality of your work as an organization.

You can also leverage the failure to motivate the entire staff. You can talk about your experience as an example: "This mistake has destroyed the reputation of our section. It is not the fault of any one individual, and as the person in charge, I take full responsibility. But I need your help to make it through this difficult time. Could I ask all of you to give it your best for another six months, so that together we can achieve something even greater that will not only make up for the mistake, but also do more good for the company than we've ever done before?" Your earnest plea may motivate and encourage your staff to work harder and come up with new ideas to improve the situation.

Do not let a failure remain a failure. Instead, make it a seed of success by finding the elements within it that will lead to greater success. Learn the lessons from each mistake, and use those lessons to climb the next step of the ladder of success.

Those who do not simply think of failure as a setback, but instead learn from it how to achieve greater success, will not be dogged by any jinxes or wretchedness. Shifting your perspective to see things in a positive light is the way to transform failures into the seeds of success.

Aiming for Infinite Development

I would like to finish this chapter with a discussion about infinite growth. Every organization or business goes through periods of success when everything it does turns out well. But everything in this world balances out, so no business or industry keeps doing extraordinarily well forever.

As is often said, businesses go through a thirty-year cycle of ups and downs, so we should be bracing ourselves for future troubles and crunches while things are going well. Knowing that a period of growth will not last forever, we should develop our business as much as we can while the period of growth lasts. This is the first piece of wisdom we need to strive for infinite development.

The second piece of wisdom that will help us is to diversify our business during a period of growth. A business usually goes through a period of rapid growth when it has a blockbuster product or some other lucrative source of income. We should use this as leverage to open up new possibilities. Whether we decide to develop a new product or open a new market, we should invest in something that will benefit the company five, ten, and twenty years down the line. We should make investments that will provide for a secure future, even if they don't bring an immediate return.

The third piece of wisdom that can help us is to think of a contingency plan for the survival of our business in case the present situation or surrounding environment completely changes. When the business is doing well, it can be quite difficult to imagine it facing a major crisis, assess how many years it could withstand such a crisis, and figure out how to survive a catastrophic situation. But we should build a concrete plan to prepare for such circumstances.

A major automobile company that has been greatly profiting by exporting automobiles may one day face a crisis if the countries that it's been selling its products to decide to stop importing cars. If this were to happen, the automaker would need to find a new market in another country or consider shifting to local production.

Another, even more serious crisis that this company may face is if people stop buying cars all together. In that case, not only would they no longer be able to sell automobiles in particular countries—they wouldn't be able to sell anywhere. If the entire world stops driving cars, there will be no demand for the company's products. This is a situation in which the main line of business that brought about the company's success suddenly and completely becomes worthless.

However absurd this scenario may sound, we should still prepare for this kind of situation. And we do this not only by making investments for the future, but also by reversing our perspective. Automobile companies, for example, need to consider what people will demand if cars one day disappear. If they imagine what the world would be like without cars, they will naturally understand that people in such a world would use transportation that either flies through the air, travels above ground and underground, or moves across the water at high speeds. The company would probably be able to envision a future in which people usually travel in their private jet or in supersonic vehicles that travel on water and under and above ground.

If people one day no longer need cars to travel on the ground but demand vehicles that can travel through the air, how will this automobile company survive? Simply selling inexpensive, energy-efficient cars will not be good enough. We are already witnessing the increasing popularity of fuel-cell-powered cars, so it's obvious that any automaker that only manufactures gasoline-fueled cars will not be able to survive in the long run.

Recent developments in the field of superconductors have already made it possible for mag-lev trains to travel in mid-air, and this field is developing by the day. An automobile company might research the applications of superconductors for their vehicles. It might even need to find a completely new source of energy and develop a product that harnesses that energy.

In short, we need to create a "survival" plan in case the main line of our current business faces a critical situation. This is how we aim for infinite development.

SEVEN

The Path to Ultimate Self-Realization

What Is Self-Realization?

We have seen a boom in the self-improvement and self-realization movement in recent years, and we can find a myriad of books on the subject of self-actualization. Some of these books accord with the laws of the universe and genuinely follow the laws of the human mind, while others ignore such spiritual laws. In any case, I believe that it is essential that we begin our exploration of self-realization by considering what exactly it is.

I would like to define self-realization as consisting of the following three elements. First, self-realization is a means of achieving human happiness. Second, self-realization is a means of creating an ideal society and a perfect world. Third, self-realization contributes to the evolution of the great universe.

Let's begin with the first idea: that self-realization is about promoting human happiness. Obviously, we do not pursue self-realization to bring misery on ourselves. We would never want to actualize our potential so that we would go bankrupt or become ill and die. We pursue self-realization because doing so improves our life.

Still, many people go the wrong way in the process of trying to realize their hopes. This is why we need the second condition, which says that our self-realization should contribute to the creation of an ideal world. Any form of self-realization that does not contribute to the betterment of the whole is not genuine. To achieve self-realization in the truest sense, it is essential that, as we pursue our personal happiness, we give something back so that we're contributing to the improvement of the society and the realization of an ideal world.

This does not mean that we should sacrifice our own happiness to bring happiness to the world. Rather, we should seek the kind of personal happiness that leads to happiness of many. This idea is expressed in the slogan I created for my organization, Happy Science: "From personal happiness to public happiness." It may sound ideal to completely disregard ourselves and work solely for the greater good, but in reality, that kind of self-sacrifice does not always help the soul grow. The purpose of our life in this world is to gain experiences that will improve our souls, so we cannot just ignore the need for soul training.

It is definitely a good thing to pursue personal happiness that enlarges our soul. However, we need to pursue our personal happiness in a way that does not get in the way of other people's self-realization. This is why we need to make sure that our self-realization contributes to the betterment of the society as a whole.

The third condition of self-realization asks us to look at our planet Earth from the grand perspective of the universe and contribute to fulfilling our purpose as a member of the human race. We need to consider the purpose of humanity as a whole in the present moment. What kind of civilization should we create? What is our mission, and how do we achieve the will of the Universe or the will of God? We need to make sure that our own ideals match this greater purpose.

Our self-realization should start with the pursuit of personal happiness, which leads to public happiness and then to global or even cosmic happiness. For those who have faith, this can be the same as realizing the happiness that God seeks.

Three Methods of Achieving Self-Realization

We achieve self-realization in a number of ways, but here, I would like to group them into three types.

First, we may achieve self-realization by doing our best on our own—that is, by making the most of our abilities as we pursue our goals. This is how diligent people reach their goals: through their own intellectual endeavors and actions. For example, if we need to take an exam, we may study on our own, at home, without asking for anyone's help. Or we may work on our own to improve our productivity at work.

Second, we may achieve self-realization by looking for more efficient and systematic ways of doing things. For example, to pass an exam, we might hire a tutor, attend a prep school, or take a correspondence course. If our goal is to install a computerized system at work, we might hire someone to assist us or outsource that part of our work. If we are having management issues, we might hire a consultant or management accountant.

This second method of achieving self-realization is about adopting rational approaches and advanced techniques. On a corporate level, it's extremely difficult *not* to do this. In a private business or small company, the person at the top may be able to do what he likes to do at his own discretion, but when a business grows to a certain size, the abilities of one person at the top are not enough to oversee all the company's functions; assessment and advice from specialists in each area become indispensable to the company's growth. This is how companies grow into corporate giants.

Third, we might achieve self-realization by finding collaborators who will support us and help us achieve our goals. With this method, we facilitate our work by gathering a group of people who share the same goals and aspirations. While the second method is about improving quality and efficiency, this method is about increasing the number of people who are willing to work together toward the same goal. For instance, a company may have specific weak areas that it wishes to beef up while expanding or developing its strengths. Using the third method, this company can partner with another company that has expertise in its weak areas. It can also employ a large number of specialists from the relevant field. By increasing the number of collaborators, any group or organization can enhance its capability. To pursue development in this way—by expanding our capacity, increasing our workforce, and collaborating with more people—we need to find capable people to help us.

This same method can work spiritually, too. We can receive help and support from a variety of guiding spirits who offer guidance to help us. That is another way of achieving self-realization.

How Self-Realization Works

As we use these methods to pursue self-realization and achieve our ideals, we take four basic steps. First, we develop an aspiration or a strong will to achieve our goal. We can think of this as having motivation, drive, or grit. Second, we envision our goal. To achieve self-realization, we need to picture our dream or our ideal self.

Third, we consider the measures we will take to reach our goal. This is where we think about which of the three methods we will use to achieve self-realization: making personal improvements by relying on our own efforts, making qualitative improvements by taking a systematic and rational approach, or making quantitative improvements by increasing our workforce. We consider the various strategies and tactics involved in each method and use that analysis to choose the best method for achieving our goal.

Finally, we create a plan for after we have achieved our goal. What will our next step be? We can progress even further in our self-realization by planning for our longer-range goals, including those that we would like to achieve a year, three years, and five years after we've achieved our first goal.

Most people limit themselves to very small goals when they think about self-realization. For example, they may wish to move to a slightly bigger house, make their business a little more lucrative, or get a salary increase. But the way we attract people to help us achieve our goal is by holding a vision of a grand dream. People are naturally drawn to those with lofty ideals; no one gathers around people whose aims are mediocre. People are not inspired by small objectives, such as increasing annual sales by 10 or 20 percent. That's why we have to have a vision of what we would like to achieve after we have achieved our first goal.

If our first goal is to increase our sales by a certain percentage, our next goal may be to invest in a new business, and the goal after that may be to construct a building for that business. Each step we take must contain within it the seeds of the next. Just like Hegel's dialectics of thesis, antithesis and synthesis, we need to take an approach that helps us move on to the next stage once we have realized our initial goal. A superficial, inflated dream won't help us achieve self-realization, but an authentic, bold, ambitious vision that inspires others is essential to self-realization.

To sum up, our first step is to have the will to achieve self-realization. Next, we need to picture our ideal and develop a clear vision of what we wish to achieve. Third, we consider which method to use to achieve our goals. Finally, we create a clear plan of what we will do after we have achieved our goals.

When we build our future plan, we should decide how we will give back to those who have helped us achieve our goals. This doesn't necessarily mean offering a monetary reward, but whatever we offer should be a stepping stone to their success— something that will help them take their next step. Achieving self-realization should not be difficult for those who can think this far ahead.

I would like to conclude this section by reminding you once again that high ideals and grand visions are what inspire and motivate people to gather around us and offer help in our pursuit of self-realization.

Avoiding Pitfalls on the Path to Self-Realization

When we are in the process of realizing our hopes, we are filled with joy and exhilaration. But we want to be careful not to fall into the pitfall of getting carried away. Devoting ourselves to our goals is not a bad thing. But immersing ourselves in our pursuit of self-realization may lead us to lose sight of ourselves and our surroundings. The risk is if we become so single-minded that we can't see approaching dangers.

We can take three precautions to avoid this pitfall. The first is to always remember our original intention. As we pursue self-realization, various new elements will come into play, such as new information and new people, and we'll have to change course to take these new elements into account. There is nothing wrong with adjusting our plan, but we have to be careful not to be blinded by initial success so that we end up neglecting our original purpose. Various events will give us second thoughts, but we should not be swayed; we should reaffirm our original intention time and again.

The most essential factor in achieving self-realization is our will or our original intention. Everything depends on how resolute our intention was, and we should not change it unless we have a very good reason for doing so. When we are tempted to change our plan or doubt our decisions, we should think about how best to carry out our original intention. Before we change our purpose, we should collect enough information to convince ourselves that we are doing it for a good reason.

A second precaution we can take is to carefully select our associates. When we are in the process of developing, we often focus on expansion and become oblivious to everything else, and we may not notice that a danger is lurking within our organization and spreading like a cancer. Preventing this starts with choosing the right associates.

Human beings are children of God and are essentially good. But human beings also have an innate desire for growth that sometimes develops into greed. We should be particularly on guard against people who offer to help us for personal gain. You may, for example, decide to partner with another company that you think can strengthen your company's weak areas and help your business expand. But if you choose the wrong business partner, that partner might end up taking over your company.

Finally, we need to guard against our own pride. Human beings tend to overestimate their own abilities and become conceited. We are prone to be contented with small successes. It is all too easy to believe people's flattery about our easy accomplishments, because it massages our ego. But allowing ourselves to be satisfied with small successes can be our downfall. The biggest trap of self-realization is conceit.

We guard against this trap by adopting a humble attitude, always speaking with humility, and behaving modestly so as not to develop too high an opinion of ourselves. We should also avoid showing off, because doing so can draw hostility and animosity. Instead, we should remain reserved in all that we do as we make steady advancements, step by step.

We need to be especially careful to avoid lavish demeanor that displays our initial achievements as transparently as if we had put them in a glass case. Showing off actually prevents us from achieving further success. We should take firm and steady steps as we climb up the ladder of success.

We also guard against pride by maintaining an attitude of devotion to the Divine. To put it another way, we give thanks for everything that is allowing us to live. Capable people who have achieved their ambitions often become overconfident in their abilities and even become arrogant. We want to avoid this, so we must always remember to have gratitude. This means being grateful to our family, friends, and clients for their support. It also means giving thanks for the bounty of animals and plants that sustain our life. Finally, we should give thanks to the underlying energy that lets us live.

These precautions can be summarized into two points, which are to maintain a humble attitude and to be grateful for what we are given. With this attitude, we can avoid traps that may hamper our self-realization.

Advanced Self-Realization

The general principles this chapter has discussed so far provide a strong groundwork for our pursuit of self-realization. But we can advance even further by making improvements in two areas: our goals and the methods we take to achieve our goals.

I recommend using the three-stage method to set your goals. I suggest creating three types of goals that you would like to achieve: small objectives, medium-sized objectives, and big objectives. Grand ideals are generally somewhat unrealistic, and we often lose sight of them and end up letting them go, while too small a goal will never lead us to great success. Specialists, experts, and artists who are highly skilled and knowledgeable in their particular field often do not achieve great success because their aims remain small. Such people have forgotten the importance of cherishing a high ambition.

But we can't achieve a big objective instantaneously. So we need to first refine our skills and build confidence in our abilities as we strive to achieve our small objectives. After that, we can start working on our medium-sized objectives and then finally move on to our big objectives. We need to climb our ladder step by step to keep advancing in our self-realization. For this reason, it is best to set all three types of objectives.

We also need to consider what methods to take to achieve our goals. To develop as an organization or improve in our operations, we need to try different approaches. We may be able to achieve our small objectives in a conventional way, but we will need new and more advanced techniques to achieve larger goals. Constructive self-realization is possible only when we keep looking for new ideas and constantly explore new methods and techniques.

Even if we have worked single-handedly to get our business off the ground, we cannot assume that it will keep developing in the same manner; we will need to delegate some management to our employees or associates. Expanding a business inevitably entails increasing and educating personnel. Otherwise, we simply become exhausted and eventually burn out.

For example, if you run a private school, no matter how good you are at teaching, you cannot handle every aspect of the school's operation yourself. As the number of students increases, you will have to hire teachers and administrative staff, and you'll need to train them so that they can take over part of your work. Not all the people you hire will have the skills they'll need to do these tasks, so educating will be vital to the development of the school. An increased workforce and investments in facilities and equipment are necessary if you are to achieve great success.

To avoid errors in judgment, remember that you are laying the foundations for greater development in the future. And be open-minded to new ideas and new ways of doing things, even if they conflict with how you have been running your business so far.

We should not change our practices too easily, but if we are to achieve advanced self-realization, we must constantly strive to improve our methods and techniques. That way, we avoid complacency: we go beyond being satisfied with our initial achievements and establish a firm footing in society to make our mark in the world.

The Ultimate Self-Realization

I would like to end this chapter with a discussion of the ultimate self-realization. The prerequisites for ultimate self-realization include the achievement of great ideals that surpass our personal self-realization, as well as accomplishments that gain us recognition for our contributions to society. But these accomplishments alone are not sufficient to achieve ultimate self-realization.

Sooner or later, our lives on earth will come to an end. We will die, leave our physical bodies, and move on to the eternal world. There is no exception to this rule. Some people do not believe in the existence of the next world, but I assure you that it truly exists.

When we return to the other world, we will not be able to take our company or property with us. What, then, do you think will remain with us when our life on earth ends? When we die, we can only bring back our soul, or the experiences and personal character that we have cultivated.

From this perspective, what is our ultimate self-realization? It all boils down to filling our soul with light. This can be measured by how well we have refined and developed our character as we have pursued self-realization. It can also be assessed by the amount of wisdom we have been able to accumulate from our experiences in this world. So the ultimate self-realization entails improving the caliber of our character and cultivating a rich stock of experiences for our spiritual growth.

When we consider self-realization from this viewpoint, another facet becomes clear—one that can be expressed by the phrase *selfless achievement of a great ambition*. This is exactly the sort of self-realization we should strive for. To be selfless means knowing that human beings are living according to the will of the great universe. It is to become aware of how small our existence is when seen from the grand perspective of the universe. It is about letting go of our ego. This is what it means to be selfless.

Our great ambition should be to achieve our highest ideal. Selfless achievement of a great ambition is about making great accomplishments while remaining humble and free from worldly obsessions. It is when we attain this state of mind that we can achieve truly great success in both the development of our character and the accumulation of precious experiences.

As we seek solutions to our management and economic problems, we need to explore and cultivate our mind. To this end, it is essential that we learn spiritual teachings that enrich our heart and mind. Only when our self-realization is backed by our self-growth will our economic development and prosperity have real significance. It is my sincere hope that many people will achieve this ultimate self-realization.

EIGHT

Success Principles for Today's Leaders

New Developments in
the Philosophy of Success

In this last chapter, I would like to discuss a new perspective on the principles of success. We can find countless books on the subject of success, and I have read many myself. But I decided to write this book because I couldn't find any that completely satisfied me. What stuck in my mind as I read through books on success was that the authors seemed not to understand the true essence of human beings and of the world. For what purpose should we achieve success? What kind or what level of success should we aim for? To answer these questions, we need to see our life from the perspective of life's true expert: God. I believe that this spiritual perspective is what the existing books on success lack.

Even in religion, we find some teachings that truly benefit us and others that actually harm our souls. The same principle holds true in the paradigm of success. Under the guise of teaching success, some books can drag us to the brink of spiritual failure.

To develop new principles of success, there is one thing we should know first and foremost, and that is to not focus solely on outcomes. Of course, achievement should accompany success. But the most important factor in success is the process of achieving it: how we live our lives. Outcomes do not necessarily determine success.

Some of the great historical figures who faced tragic ends might be considered failures if their lives were assessed solely based on their worldly achievements. But if we look at their process—how they lived their lives—we see that many of them achieved great success despite their unfortunate ends.

The principles of success are not only about the results we attain. We need to consider how we live our lives, whether we are filling ourselves with light as we work to achieve success. And it is all the more wonderful if those shining with light can accomplish great things, wield great influence, and help many others live their lives to the fullest. Thus, the first point of my philosophy of success is that we should not become completely result-oriented, but instead become process-oriented.

My second point is to always remember to maintain a pure mind. Success should not warp our mind. Our desire for success should not make us willing to use underhanded methods to achieve our goals. We may be able to achieve temporary success with deceptive acts, but we will pay for it miserably sooner or later. We may fall into a trap or be betrayed by our colleagues. What's more, if we keep finagling, our face will turn cunning, and our entire body will take on an air of deviousness.

We must never use underhanded, deceitful, or fraudulent means to achieve success. We should instead remain true to ourselves as we seek the path to success. Our success should not deteriorate our human nature. It will serve us to stay honest, even if doing so may seem to keep success at a distance.

Rather than only seeking results, we should focus on the process of reaching our goals, and pursue whatever success that process brings us. This means living true to our heart and our conscience. It will serve us best if we can achieve success while maintaining a pure heart and remaining as innocent as a small child.

Developing Character

One important aspect of success that we should never neglect is the development of our character. I believe that the principles of success should help us not only improve our management skills and achieve economic prosperity, but also grow as human beings so that we can cultivate a sparkling, magnanimous character. As we climb the ladder of success and become leaders, we gain more influence over others, and that's why we should aim to become versatile and noble people.

How should we go about developing our inner qualities? I have touched on the importance of improving our skills, but competency is only one element of success. Competency is certainly one of the qualities we need to achieve success, but that's not all there is to it.

Our competency is our efficiency or skill; it is our ability to handle a task within a set period of time. We have a better chance of succeeding if we are competent, but success requires more than ability. In fact, becoming preoccupied with developing our ability has three possible drawbacks.

First, we may find it increasingly difficult to work in harmony with others when we focus solely on developing our competency. When our own advancement becomes our prime concern, we may gradually lose interest in the happiness of other people. We may even start to believe that we can become happy at other people's expense. As a result, we may become uncooperative and find ourselves unable to work with others.

The second risk of focusing on competency is that it may actually stand in the way of success. In the United States, getting an MBA from a prestigious university used to be a sure path to a management position, and this was once considered the best way to reach the top. But recently, the situation has changed. People are starting to realize that those who studied management at top business schools do not necessarily do well in management positions.

For instance, new MBA graduates from Harvard University would get a vice-president post at a corporation and then implement Harvard's business theories in real-life business situations. But this often caused friction with the people they worked with. These ideas might lead to success, but in implementing them, people often neglected the idea that corporations are also human societies, that they are like villages that human beings live in. It becomes problematic when the company seems to be taking on a life of its own, neglecting the human beings who work inside it.

Learning management theories or principles is not enough to bring out success on a large scale; we need to examine our inner world and understand the human mind. Recruiting people solely based on their abilities could actually prevent them from achieving greater success in life.

The third risk of focusing on our own competency is that we may become arrogant. Pride itself is not a negative trait, but it can harm us spiritually when we become too proud of ourselves. When we explore why there's so much evil in the world and how negative vibrations have become so rampant, we find that the root cause is modern people's arrogance. When we give our pride free rein, it causes various conflicts and brings harm to other people. Arrogance is like a decoration that makes us look good on the outside, like the painting on a car or a sign on a building, but it also damages the purity of our heart.

These are the three risks of choosing people based solely on their competency. We should look for those who are competent and who at the same time have a magnanimous heart, who enrich others' hearts and who quench others' thirst like an oasis. I believe the purpose of a philosophy of modern success is to produce many people who achieve economic prosperity with a big and rich heart.

The Qualities of Leadership

Assuming that many of my readers are corporate employees, I would like to talk about the qualities of leadership required for company managers. Being a leader in a corporate setting means taking a higher post than others, from assistant manager, manager, director, executive director, and president all the way to CEO. To discuss leadership, I'm calling all these positions "management."

To reach a management position, we need to meet the following three conditions. First, leaders must be capable of making difficult decisions. They have to have a strong ability to make good decisions to be able to reach the right conclusions. Second, leaders need to play a role of an educator who can train and guide subordinates. Third, leaders need to consider the financial situations of their subordinates. They need to be able to understand their influence over other people's happiness and carefully and appropriately adjust employees' salaries and bonuses.

These three abilities—decision making, training and education, and proper adjustment of employees' salaries—are required for those in managerial positions, and these also serve as criteria for measuring our leadership capability.

The first condition, being capable of making high-level, difficult decisions, requires leaders to be competent; they need strong expertise in their job. But I'm not going to delve into the topic of developing our competency in this book, because I'm sure that most people are aware that this is an essential leadership ability that they need to cultivate, and many corporations probably offer training to help employees develop this skill.

Another crucial ability that leaders need is foresight. Many people can produce results within a time frame of six months or a year, but some of these people are only interested in doing well in their current post and may not contribute to the company's long-term growth. Employees whose main concern is to achieve results that will benefit them during their tenure don't care about what happens to the company after they leave their posts, even if their actions during their tenure end up hurting the company. People like this would promise their clients future returns to gain immediate profits. They would do whatever it takes to make a profitable deal during their tenure and leave their successors all kinds of problems to take care of. These people cause trouble for the company and the people who come after them.

We are evaluated based on our performance in our current post, so we do need to achieve solid results to earn a raise or promotion. And we can certainly argue that there is something wrong with this way of assessing people's abilities. Still, it is important to know that our overall competency or job performance will improve when we do our job in a way that will benefit the areas that are not directly connected to our personal performance.

We can allocate 60 to 70 percent of our time to tasks that directly contribute to our personal performance, but we should use the remaining 30 to 40 percent to lay the groundwork for those who come after us and to contribute to the development of the company. We should always keep these twin goals in mind as we engage in our day-to-day work.

The second condition of leadership—developing our capacity as an educator—is often undervalued. In general, the ability to train and educate others is not as appreciated as competency at one's job is. In fact, competent people often immerse themselves in advancing their career, even at the cost of others, while educators who can nurture and guide others often fall behind in the rat race and end up in unimportant positions. Corporations should be a training ground for character building and should highlight and value educational skill in their leaders. This ability to teach and guide others will be increasingly demanded and valued in the coming age.

What conditions do leaders need to meet to serve as educators? First, they need expertise so they can teach those who work under them. Second, they need a good understanding of human beings. We can't teach others or bring out the best in them unless we get to know them deeply. Leaders need expertise in both the area of their work and the human mind. So if we want to advance into a managerial position, we need to develop a breadth of knowledge about human beings and broaden the scope of our experiences.

Third, leaders need to understand that managers hold the keys to the financial situations of their subordinates. They are in the influential position of evaluating others' performances and deciding whether they deserve a raise, a promotion, or an increase in their bonus. So it is no exaggeration to say that others' economic well-being depends on the decisions that managers make.

Managers must realize that they have the power to influence others' economic happiness and must always strive to evaluate others fairly and with dignity and piety, as if they are answering God's will. They should never evaluate others based on their personal likes and dislikes.

Impartiality is not something we learn only in school and through social training. We foster a spirit of fairness when we seek Right Mind, which we can cultivate by learning and understanding spiritual teachings that come from higher dimensions in heaven. We need to remain humble, respectful, and devoted to the Divine. Evaluating others is indeed sacred work. A nonjudgmental attitude is a must for leaders who are in a position to significantly affect others' well-being.

The Qualities of a Successful Business Owner

In the previous section, I discussed the qualities and conditions necessary for managers in a corporate environment. I would now like to talk about the essential conditions for business owners and entrepreneurs who start and run their own business.

I believe that there are three prerequisites for running a successful business. The first is to have a good sense of balance. Business owners need this ability in two areas: financial affairs and personnel affairs. They need a good sense of balance to manage income and expenses and to recruit employees and assign them to appropriate posts.

When we hire the right people for the right job, their potential can develop infinitely. But if we assign them to a job that they are not suited for, they will not be able to use their abilities at all. Maintaining a balance in human resource management is about placing the staff in a way that enhances the overall performance of the company. This balance of personnel is related to balancing revenue and expenditures; both are about looking at the whole picture and considering all the parts equally.

The second essential condition for becoming a successful business owner is to be future-oriented. This means foreseeing what will happen one, five, or ten years from now. We need to anticipate not only the future of our own company, but also the business prospects of fields outside our own industry. We need to look toward the future and explore our options and possibilities for further prosperity.

Business owners must have a perspective that transcends the past, present, and future. When we look to the past, we consider the starting point of our business and review where the company stands, its role in society, and its operations in the present. When we look to the future, we see how our business will develop and comprehensively determine the personnel, funds, and space we will need to make this vision come true.

We will be able to see beyond the past, present, and future when we gain an objective perspective, as if we are looking at ourselves through the eyes of another. The key to gaining this time-transcending perspective is to detach our consciousness and see things objectively, going beyond what our physical eyes can see. It is as if our consciousness leaves our physical bodies, rises high above the sky, and looks down at ourselves on earth. Leaders should not be blinded by their emotions; they should be able to look at themselves and their surroundings objectively.

The third prerequisite for becoming a successful business owner is to constantly strive to be of service to the world. We can achieve some degree of success even if we focus only on making profits to benefit our company or for our personal gain. But this type of success will not last; we will eventually trip and fall some way or another. Owners of a thriving business are blessed with success and are in an advantageous position in society, and that success gives them the duty to give back to society. Only people who are committed to serving the greater good should qualify as top leaders of organizations.

While the second condition is about having a perspective that transcends time, the third condition is about having a perspective that transcends space. Top-level leaders need to be able to see themselves within the contexts of the industry, the society, the country, and the entire world.

Returning the Love We Receive

The third essential condition of those in leadership positions is realizing that it is our duty, as members of society, to give back to society. Put more simply, it is our duty to return the love we receive. We must always be looking for ways to repay love and circulate it back to society.

As I have mentioned, gratitude is vitally important to success in life. We want to accomplish great things, like starting and operating a new business, taking on a new leadership position, and becoming widely recognized in society—but we cannot accomplish these things on our own. Self-reliance is not the only quality we need to reach a managerial or executive position in a corporation. Getting to these places requires the dedicated support and cooperation of many people around us. If our subordinates, superiors, colleagues, and others around us are dissatisfied with our work, it will not be possible for us to successfully manage other employees or to head a whole organization. What's more, each of these people's support is indispensable to the ultimate success of our work and enterprise.

When we reach upper-level positions, it is important to remember all the hard work that those around us put in to making our achievements possible. If we truly appreciate the love we have received from others, we naturally want to give something back to them in return. As we continue to take on more advanced positions and statuses, we should feel an even stronger desire to give back even greater amounts of love.

This lasting gratitude of the heart, I believe, is the mark of one who will reach true success.

Personifying Love

Another way to think about giving back is to think about taking the love we feel inside us, developing it, and expressing it outwardly in our actions.

In *The Laws of the Sun*, I described love as consisting developmental stages that serve as vital measures of our growth as human beings. These stages consist, chiefly, of fundamental love, spiritually nurturing love, forgiving love, and love incarnate.

The first stage of love, fundamental love, is one step above instinctive love. While instinctive love is mostly about receiving love from others, fundamental love is about *giving* love to others. In short, we are capable of fundamental love when our state of mind has progressed enough to give and serve others, as opposed to just receiving.

When our desire to give and serve others advances further, we become capable of the next stage: spiritually nurturing love. This stage is defined by the love that we administer through our leadership, and it is a love based on the desire to nurture people, organizations, and societies as a whole.

When our love progresses to the next stage, we begin to see the world from a spiritual perspective. This is the stage of forgiving love. If nurturing love is a love we give to those who work under our guidance and leadership, forgiving love is a kind of love that we give impartially to everyone. It is void of favoritism and discrimination. It sees everyone as born of the same roots and approaches all people as equal brothers and sisters. In short, forgiving love is a state of mind that notices but transcends the good and evil in others.

The final stage is love incarnate. Love incarnate is the kind of love embodied by people of such greatness that they become the spirit of their age. Their very presence in this world becomes an advent of love itself. Their love cannot necessarily be recognized as tangible deeds or actions. Rather, they personify love and express love in their whole being. They are pure embodiments of the idea we call love.

This stage of love is not totally out of our reach. Our hearts are capable of a simple version of love incarnate. Whether we are at work or at home, we can personify love by striving to be someone that others feel happy to know. When we practice love incarnate, others appreciate our presence in their lives; they feel happy to have met us, lived with us, or worked with us. It is my hope that many of my readers will advance to these examples of love incarnate.

The Bible teaches that fame and status are futile if they are not accompanied by love: "Whoever does not love does not know God, for God is love" (1 John 4:8). In the same way, whoever achieves success but does not love does not know true success. We must put effort into cultivating greater love toward the goal of achieving the state of love incarnate. This effort to love is essential to true success.

This book has described various facets of my principles of success. What sums them all up is this quality of love. I feel that the unceasing practice of evolving the love in our hearts is indispensable to a philosophy of modern success. In the final analysis, the culmination of this philosophy lies in the progress of our love through these developmental stages and, to be more specific, the attainment of the state of love incarnate. I believe that we are only truly successful when we arrive at this stage. A deep and exalted love is the ultimate method of achieving true success.

AFTERWORD

Can there be any other book so overwhelmingly full of light? Have you read any work that inspires as much courage and hope as this? Can anything else compare with its power to inspirit you when you are in the midst of a failure, setbacks, anxiety, or feelings of inferiority?

In times of heartbreak, unemployment, severe illness, setbacks in college admissions, crumbling family relationships, problems in other relationships, and anxieties about growing older, these pages will give you the light of guidance.

Your belief in this book will make your dreams come true.
This book is your beacon of light through times of hardship and sorrow.
You must believe in this miraculous work.

If you are lying in distress in a hospital bed or facing an illness in your family, I hope that you will read a little bit of this book each day to serve as your wellspring of courage and nourishment for your soul. As you do, I am certain that the conditions you face will take a turn for the better, allowing your family to restore its precious cheer and joy.

Ryuho Okawa
Founder and CEO
Happy Science Group

ABOUT THE AUTHOR

RYUHO OKAWA is Global Visionary, renowned spiritual leader, and best-selling author in Japan with a simple goal: to help people find true happiness and create a better world.

His deep compassion and sense of responsibility for the happiness of each individual has prompted him to publish over 2,100 titles of religious, spiritual, and self-development teachings, covering a broad range of topics including how our thoughts influence reality, the nature of love, and the path to enlightenment. He also writes on the topics of management and economy, as well as the relationship between religion and politics in the global context. To date, Okawa's books have sold over 100 million copies worldwide and been translated into 28 languages.

Okawa has dedicated himself to improving society and creating a better world. In 1986, Okawa founded Happy Science as a spiritual movement dedicated to bringing greater happiness to humankind by uniting religions and cultures to live in harmony. Happy Science has grown rapidly from its beginnings in Japan to a worldwide organization with over twelve million members. Okawa is compassionately committed to the spiritual growth of others. In addition to writing and publishing books, he continues to give lectures around the world.

ABOUT HAPPY SCIENCE

Happy Science is a global movement that empowers individuals to find purpose and spiritual happiness and to share that happiness with their families, societies, and the world. With more than twelve million members around the world, Happy Science aims to increase awareness of spiritual truths and expand our capacity for love, compassion, and joy so that together we can create the kind of world we all wish to live in.

Activities at Happy Science are based on the Principles of Happiness (Love, Wisdom, Self-Reflection, and Progress). These principles embrace worldwide philosophies and beliefs, transcending boundaries of culture and religions.

Love teaches us to give ourselves freely without expecting anything in return; it encompasses giving, nurturing, and forgiveness.

Wisdom leads us to the insights of spiritual truths, and opens us to the true meaning of life and the will of God (the universe, the highest power, Buddha).

Self-Reflection brings a mindful, nonjudgmental lens to our thoughts and actions to help us find our truest selves—the essence of our souls—and deepen our connection to the highest power. It helps us attain a clean and peaceful mind and leads us to the right life path.

Progress emphasizes the positive, dynamic aspects of our spiritual growth—actions we can take to manifest and spread happiness around the world. It's a path that not only expands our soul growth, but also furthers the collective potential of the world we live in.

PROGRAMS AND EVENTS

The doors of Happy Science are open to all. We offer a variety of programs and events, including self-exploration and self-growth programs, spiritual seminars, meditation and contemplation sessions, study groups, and book events.

Our programs are designed to:

- Deepen your understanding of your purpose and meaning in life
- Improve your relationships and increase your capacity to love unconditionally
- Attain a peace of mind, decrease anxiety and stress, and feel positive
- Gain deeper insights and a broader perspective on the world
- Learn how to overcome life's challenges
  ... and much more.

For more information, visit happyscience-na.org or happy-science.org.

INTERNATIONAL SEMINARS

Each year, friends from all over the world join our international seminars, held at our faith centers in Japan. Different programs are offered each year and cover a wide variety of topics, including improving relationships, practicing the Eightfold Path to enlightenment, and loving yourself, to name just a few.

HAPPY SCIENCE MONTHLY

Our monthly publication covers the latest featured lectures, members' life-changing experiences and other news from members around the world, book reviews, and many other topics. Downloadable PDF files are available at happyscience-na. org. Copies and back issues in Portuguese, Chinese, and other languages are available upon request. For more information, contact us via e-mail at tokyo@happy-science.org.

CONTACT INFORMATION

Happy Science is a worldwide organization with faith centers around the globe. For a comprehensive list of centers, visit the worldwide directory at happy-science.org or happyscience-na. org. The following are some of the many Happy Science locations:

UNITED STATES AND CANADA

NEW YORK

79 Franklin Street
New York, NY 10013
Phone: 212-343-7972
Fax: 212-343-7973
Email: ny@happy-science.org
Website: newyork.happyscience-na.org

SAN FRANCISCO

525 Clinton Street
Redwood City, CA 94062
Phone/Fax: 650-363-2777
Email: sf@happy-science.org
Website: sanfrancisco.happyscience-na.org

FLORIDA

5208 8th St.
Zephyrhills, FL 33542
Phone: 813-715-0000
Fax: 813-715-0010
Email: florida@happy-science.org
Website: florida.happyscience-na.org

NEW JERSEY

725 River Rd., #102B
Edgewater, NJ 07020
Phone: 201-313-0127
Fax: 201-313-0120
Email: nj@happy-science.org
Website: newjersey.happyscience-na.org

ATLANTA

1874 Piedmont Ave. NE Suite 360-C
Atlanta, GA 30324
Phone: 404-892-7770
Email: atlanta@happy-science.org
Website: atlanta.happyscience-na.org

LOS ANGELES

1590 E. Del Mar Blvd.
Pasadena, CA 91106
Phone: 626-395-7775
Fax: 626-395-7776
Email: la@happy-science.org
Website: losangeles.happyscience-na.org

ORANGE COUNTY

10231 Slater Ave., #204
Fountain Valley, CA 92708
Phone: 714-745-1140
Email: oc@happy-science.org

SAN DIEGO

Email: sandiego@happy-science.org

HAWAII

1221 Kapiolani Blvd., Suite 920
Honolulu, HI 96814
Phone: 808-591-9772
Fax: 808-591-9776
Email: hi@happy-science.org
Website: hawaii.happyscience-na.org

KAUAI

4504 Kukui Street
Dragon Building, Suite 21
Kapaa, HI 96746
Phone: 808-822-7007
Fax: 808-822-6007
Email: kauai-hi@happy-science.org
Website: kauai.happyscience-na.org

TORONTO

323 College Street
Toronto, ON M5T 1S2 Canada
Phone/Fax: 1-416-901-3747
Email: toronto@happy-science.org
Website: happy-science.ca

VANCOUVER

#212-2609 East 49th Avenue
Vancouver, BC, V5S 1J9 Canada
Phone: 1-604-437-7735
Fax: 1-604-437-7764
Email: vancouver@happy-science.org
Website: happy-science.ca

INTERNATIONAL

TOKYO

1-6-7 Togoshi, Shinagawa
Tokyo, 142-0041 Japan
Phone: 81-3-6384-5770
Fax: 81-3-6384-5776
Email: tokyo@happy-science.org
Website: happy-science.org

LONDON

3 Margaret Street
London, W1W 8RE United Kingdom
Phone: 44-20-7323-9255
Fax: 44-20-7323-9344
Email: eu@happy-science.org
Website: happyscience-uk.org

SYDNEY

516 Pacific Hwy Lane Cove North,
NSW 2066 Australia
Phone: 61-2-9411-2877
Fax: 61-2-9411-2822
Email: sydney@happy-science.org

BRAZIL HEADQUARTERS

Rua. Domingos de Morais 1154,Vila Mariana,
Sao Paulo, CEP 04009-002 Brazil
Phone: 55-11-5088-3800
Fax: 55-11-5088-3806
Email: sp@happy-science.org
Website: cienciadafelicidade.com.br

JUNDIAI

Rua Congo, 447, Jd.Bonfiglioli,
Jundiai, CEP 13207-340
Phone: 55-11-4587-5952
Email: jundiai@happy-sciece.org

SEOUL

74, Sadang-ro 27-gil, Dongjak-gu, Seoul, Korea
Phone: 82-2-3478-8777
Fax: 82-2-3478-9777
Email: korea@happy-science.org
Website: happyscience-korea.org

TAIPEI

No. 89, Lane 155, Dunhua N. Road
Songshan District, Taipei City 105 Taiwan
Phone: 886-2-2719-9377
Fax: 886-2-2719-5570
Email: taiwan@happy-science.org
Website: happyscience-tw.org

MALAYSIA

No 22A, Block2, Jalil Link, Jalan Jalil Jaya 2, Bukit Jalil 57000,
Kuala Lumpur, Malaysia
Phone: 60-3-8998-7877
Fax: 60-3-8998-7977
Email: malaysia@happy-science.org
Website: happyscience.org.my

NEPAL

Kathmandu Metropolitan City,
Ward No. 15, Ring Road, Kimdol, Sitapaila,
Kathmandu, Nepal
Phone: 977-1-427-2931
Email: nepal@happy-science.org

UGANDA

Plot 877 Rubaga Road, Kampala P.O. Box 34130
Kampala, Uganda
Phone: 256-79-3238-002
Email: uganda@happy-science.org
Website: happyscience-uganda.org

ABOUT IRH PRESS USA INC.

IRH Press USA Inc. was founded in 2013 as an affiliated firm of IRH Press Co., Ltd. Based in New York, the press publishes books in various categories including spirituality, religion, and self-improvement and publishes books by Ryuho Okawa, the author of 100 million books sold worldwide. For more information, visit OkawaBooks.com.

FOLLOW US ON:

Facebook: MasterOkawaBooks

Twitter: OkawaBooks

Goodreads: RyuhoOkawa

Instagram: OkawaBooks

Pinterest: OkawaBooks

BOOKS BY RYUHO OKAWA

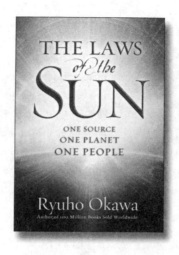

THE LAWS OF THE SUN
One Source, One Planet, One People

Hardcover | 264 pages | $24.95 | ISBN: 978-1937673-04-8

IMAGINE IF YOU COULD ASK GOD why He created this world and what spiritual laws He used to shape us—and everything around us. In *The Laws of the Sun*, Okawa outlines these laws of the universe and provides a road map for living one's life with greater purpose and meaning. This powerful book shows the way to realize true happiness—a happiness that continues from this world through the other.

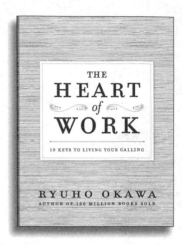

THE HEART OF WORK
10 Keys to Living Your Calling

Softcover | 224 pages | $12.95
ISBN: 978-1942125-03-7

Ryuho Okawa shares 10 key principles that will help you get to the heart of work, manage your time well, prioritize your work, live with long health and vitality, achieve growth, and more. People of all walks of life—from the businessperson, executive, artist, teacher, mother, to even students—will find the keys to achieving happiness and success in their special calling.

THINK BIG!
Be Positive and Be Brave
to Achieve Your Dreams

Softcover | 160 pages | $12.95
ISBN: 978-1-942125-04-4

This self-development book offers practical steps to consciously create a life of rewarding challenge, fulfillment, and achievement. Ryuho Okawa inspires us with practical steps for building courage, choosing a constructive perspective, finding a true calling, cultivating awareness, and harnessing our personal power to realize our dreams.

A LIFE OF TRIUMPH
Unleashing Your Light Upon the World

THE MIRACLE OF MEDITATION
Opening Your Life to Peace, Joy, and the Power Within

THE ESSENCE OF BUDDHA
The Path to Enlightenment

THE LAWS OF JUSTICE
How We Can Solve World Conflicts and Bring Peace

INVITATION TO HAPPINESS
7 Inspirations from Your Inner Angel

MESSAGES FROM HEAVEN
What Jesus, Buddha, Muhammad, and Moses Would Say Today

SECRETS OF
THE EVERLASTING TRUTHS
A New Paradigm for Living on Earth

THE NINE DIMENSIONS
Unveiling the Laws of Eternity

THE MOMENT OF TRUTH
Become a Living Angel Today

CHANGE YOUR LIFE,
CHANGE THE WORLD
A Spiritual Guide to Living Now

For a complete list of books, visit OkawaBooks.com.